Prayers and thoughts of Chinese Christians

Presented by Kim-Kwong Chan and Alan Hunter

Property of
INSTITUTE FOR WORSHIP STUDIES
Orange Park, Florida

Cowley Publications

Published in the United States of America by **Cowley Publications**
28 Temple Place, Boston, MA 02111

Published in Great Britain by Mowbray, a Cassell imprint

Translations and editorial material
© Kim-Kwong Chan and Alan Hunter 1991

All rights reserved. No part of this manuscript may be reproduced or transmitted in any form or by any means, electronic or mechanical including photocopying, recording or any information storage or retrieval system, without prior permission in writing from the publishers.

First published 1991

Library of Congress Cataloging-in-Publication Data
Prayers and thoughts of Chinese Christians/presented by Kim-Kwong Chan and Alan Hunter
      p.   cm.
  Includes bibliographical references.
  ISBN 1-56101-039-1
  1. Christians—China. 2. Christianity—China—History.
3. Communism and Christianity—China—History—20th Century.
4. Persecution—China—History—20th century. 5. China—Politics and government—1949–   I. Chan, Kim-Kwong, 1958–   II. Hunter, Alan, 1951–
BR1288.P73   1991   91–7284
275. 1—dc20   CIP

Typeset by Litho Link Ltd, Welshpool, Powys, Wales

Printed and bound in Great Britain by Biddles Ltd, Guildford and King's Lynn

Contents

Acknowledgements	vi
Introduction	1
Perseverance in suffering	17
Moral conduct	31
Christocentric devotion	37
Nationalism	53
Cultural continuity	59
Evangelism	68
Longer articles	
'Give ye them to eat'	76
The goal of the Gospel	81
A Christian village	93
Set apart	97
Two prayers after the events of 4 June 1989	102
Statement by hunger strikers in Tiananmen Square	103
Recommended reading	104

I think the book is splendid — the best thing in this department that I have seen for a long time . . . the book is so alert . . . I find on re-reading it that much of the material is very far from conventional.

David Paton

Praise to the Father

We worship You, great, holy and merciful Father who have the beauteous face of the sun and moon.
Your towering merit transcends all the saints.
Your Word and Truth are golden treasures.
Your grace is given to all.
We have been corrupted by sin and lost our true nature.
Only our Lord Jesus, who lives in eternal transcendence, incarnated onto the dusty earth to cast out evil demons for the benefit of humanity.
You use Your truth to govern us with benevolence.
We praise You in peace and honesty because You, our Holy Father, use Your mighty power to save us.
Your might is beyond all comprehension.
May all glory and praise belong to the Holy Trinity.
Salute to the Apostle St John.

Shu Yuan, a Nestorian in China, wrote this prayer of praise in the ninth century.

Acknowledgements

No. 61 is taken from *The Normal Christian Life* by Watchman Nee, © Angus I. Kinnear 1957, published by Gospel Literature Service, Bombay, India; revised edition 1969, by permission of Kingsway Publications Ltd, 1 St Anne's Road, Eastbourne BN21 3UN; G. R. Welch Co. Ltd, 960 Gateway, Burlington, Ontario L7L 5K7; and Tyndale House Publishers Inc., 351 Executive Drive, Wheaton, Illinois 60189–0080. All rights reserved.
Nos 62 and 63 are taken from *Households of God on China's Soil*, compiled and translated by Raymond Fung, © World Council of Churches, Geneva, Switzerland 1982, by permission of World Council of Churches.

Introduction

It is a surprise, if one is not prepared, to come across Christianity in China — like seeing a familar face in an unexpected situation. And as one reads, or perhaps has the opportunity to see at first hand, new revelations occur. Christianity is not only where one might expect to find it, in Westernized Hong Kong or Taiwan; it exists in remote mountain provinces, in the heart of the Communist cities, in labour camps. The language is indeed different; but prayers, hymns, and letters, carry a similar message in every language. Christianity has long been established in Europe, but it also finds a home in the East. It seems to speak to human beings in a way that transcends nations and cultures. When you meet Chinese Christianity you meet a stranger and an old friend at the same time.

Yet we should not be too surprised. The division between East and West, Europe and Asia, is not eternal. Before the consolidation of national identities the world was in some senses less fragmented, and it was in this neglected period of history that Christianity reached China. In the fifth and sixth centuries AD, Central Asia was the seat of a highly developed culture. The great plains around the city of Samarkand were inhabited by Indo-European peoples who had strong links with the Persian religion of Zoroastrianism, but they were increasingly influenced by Christianity. Further, Samarkand was the most important city on the Silk Road, that fascinating 5,000-mile route that ran from Antioch on the Mediterranean to Chang'an (Xi'an), Imperial city of China. Along the road travelled merchants and adventurers, diplomats and priests, all contributing to the exchange of goods, ideas and inventions.

In 635 a Persian missionary, Aloben, arrived in Chang'an. As far as we know this was the first occasion when Christianity made an impact on the Imperial Court. Aloben was well received and his religion was honoured in an Imperial edict of 638:

> The monk Aloben from Persia has come from afar with the Scriptures and the doctrines; we find this religion excellent and separate from the world, and acknowledge that it is quickening for mankind and indispensable. It succours human beings, is beneficial to the human race and is worthy of being spread all over the Celestial Empire.

Christianity was virtually eliminated by purges later in the Tang Dynasty (late ninth century), but this episode provides insight into a dynamic period of cultural exchange. Another little-known fact is that Genghis Khan and his Mongol troops were profoundly influenced by Christianity, and that the Nestorian Church flourished in the lands under their control. After the Mongol invasion of China in 1215, a Christian theological school and church were established in Beijing in 1235, and a century later there were reports of 30,000 Christians in China — mostly among the ruling invaders rather than native Chinese. During this period there was also a Franciscan mission to China, and formal contacts between the Pope and the Emperor. This group of Christians was virtually eliminated after the Mongols were overthrown in 1368.

It is interesting to speculate how the whole course of world history might have been very different had Christianity taken root in China through these early contacts. Would China have evolved its Celestial Empire in the same way? What would have been the relation between the Confucian classics and the Bible? Would the history of Western colonialism have been different? As it turned out, the first Christians to make a permanent impact on China, the Jesuit missionaries, arrived at the end of the sixteenth century. They were well received at court because of their mathematical and astronomical skills, their grasp of Chinese traditional culture, and their tact when dealing with Chinese customs.

Until 1720 Jesuits held important positions at court, often gaining personal audiences with the Emperor, and once again it seemed possible that Christianity would become influential at the highest levels of Chinese society. This time the process did not come to fruition because of the so-called 'Rites Controversy'. Briefly, the Pope was unwilling to tolerate any compromise with the Confucian tradition, and, much against the wishes of the Jesuits, issued edicts condemning Confucianism and ancestor worship. The Chinese emperor Kangxi, who had been an earnest supporter of Christianity, felt obliged to ban the religion in 1721. For the next hundred years Christianity survived, but believers were forced to practise their religion underground, persecuted and isolated: the chance of converting the Empire had been lost for ever. The Vatican reversed these earlier rulings in 1939.

The Jesuit mission, despite its limited success in the longer term, served many important functions, of which we can mention two. In the first place it opened a serious debate between Christianity and Chinese culture. This had a profound impact both in China and Europe. Confucians were able to approach the new doctrine through study of the excellent translation of the Scriptures made by the Jesuits and their collaborators, and the first attempts were made at mutual understanding and criticism. Equally, Europe was tremendously influenced by the impact of Chinese political, philosophical and aesthetic ideas. Confucius was called 'the patron saint of the Enlightenment', Leibniz studied Chinese mathematics, and Chinoiserie affected art and design. Secondly, despite the persecutions, devoted communities of Christians survived in many areas of China, and some Christian communities even today can trace their ancestry back to the seventeenth century. To these people Christianity is not an alien way of life, it has been in their families for hundreds of years — longer, for example, than amongst most African peoples.

In the middle of the nineteenth century the great missionary enterprise began. Until 1949 thousands of missionaries, from the USA, France, Italy, Germany, Britain and other countries devoted years of their lives to China. Many felt a strong calling to spread the Gospel there. Many were engaged in medicine, education, rural development and social work of all kinds. Some lost their lives to disease or bandits; others acquired a profound knowledge of Chinese language and culture. For a century these missionaries performed a vital role as interpreters of the West to China, and moreover as interpreters of China to the West. Most of them were obliged to report back to their home organizations and some wrote books or articles. The reading public in the West gleaned much of its knowledge of China through this channel.

There were negative sides to this enterprise, however, to which some of the missionaries and their churches remained almost entirely blind. Missionaries were by and large not welcomed with open arms by the Chinese. They were inevitably linked in the Chinese mind with soldiers, opium traders and merchants, and perceived as exploiters, hypocrites or imperialists. The missionaries often associated with the lowest classes of Chinese society, helping beggars and orphans; the Chinese elite regarded this as absurd or degrading. They also associated with merchants and landlords, earning equal distrust from the working classes. A factor that aroused particular resentment was that foreigners, and often those associated with them, were immune to the normal processes of Chinese law. Representatives of the imperial powers could literally get away with murder, and sometimes did. It was strongly suspected that the majority of Chinese Christians were converted simply because they wanted to share in the power and wealth of the Western governments rather than from purely religious motives. These people became known as 'rice-bowl' Christians and were despised by most of their compatriots.

Nevertheless Christians of all persuasions, both Protestants and Catholics, established churches and communities throughout China, often with schools, hospitals and even universities attached. Until 1949 Christianity was an undeniable aspect of the Chinese scene, particularly in the cities most exposed to Western influence, the great trading ports of the south-east. Estimates suggest that by 1949 there were around 3 million Chinese Catholics and 1 million Protestants: not a large part of the Chinese population of 450 millions, perhaps, but none the less a significant number of people with a large proportion of well-educated city dwellers. A major weakness in the situation was the churches' over-dependence on foreign bodies. A few indigenous groups had sprung up — for example the True Jesus church and the Little Flock — but on the whole the priests, pastors, missionaries, doctors and educators connected with the

Christian movement were European or American. The process of building a truly indigenous church was just beginning to seem a possibility, even if far off, when the whole enterprise was suddenly faced with a totally new set of ground rules — those determined by the Chinese Communist Party when it took power in 1949 after many years of war.

Of course Christianity did not operate in a spiritual vacuum, and it was only one element among many in Chinese religious life. The Chinese people have a rich and varied religious heritage, ranging from popular cults and folklore to sophisticated philosophies. The oldest elements have their roots in peasant cultures of antiquity, while others are products of a highly refined elite, influenced by poetry and meditation.

Popular religion profoundly influenced society throughout China for thousands of years. Every district had its own particular traditions, practices and beliefs. There was diversity in detail, but researchers have suggested that three elements were widespread, namely practices connected with gods, ghosts and ancestors. All over China local deities made up a varied pantheon from which the believer was free to choose. Gods included the spirits of local heroes, versions of Taoist or Buddhist deities, and local or animistic spirits. Particular gods were sometimes propitiated by members of particular professions, e.g. sailors or firework manufacturers. Celebrations of the gods often took the form of colourful festivals and processions. A less attractive aspect was that, as in many peasant societies, people were often frightened of ghosts and malevolent spirits, and often turned to exorcism in attempts to cure illness. Childhood diseases in particular were thought to be caused by possession. Ancestor worship was most common in South China where it played a central role in kinship, lineage and clan systems. Ancestors were thought to bring prosperity provided that descendants protected their graves and performed appropriate ceremonies. Most households had a small altar where respects would be paid to previous generations.

Among the common people great emphasis was laid on practicality. Ancestors and gods were expected to answer petitions, often for health, wealth or male offspring. If they failed to do so, the supplicant was perfectly entitled to switch allegiance to others. Temples were often dedicated to several different gods, and there was little concept of exclusivity. The entire system was decentralized, unsupervised and subject to local conditions. The complexities of ritual and divination gave rise to religious specialists such as monks, shamans, diviners, mediums, ritual leaders, astrologers and healers, who played an important role in traditional life. Many of them were obviously charlatans who were treated with contempt. Others became famous and influential locally and even nationally: popular revolts often had links with quasi-religious figures.

This network of popular religious practices has been evaluated very differently by outside observers. For some scientifically-minded Chinese, concerned with the modernization of their society, it is merely superstition, evidence of backwardness, to be discouraged as far as possible. Others, including some Western anthropologists, take a more positive view, and point to the social functions of this kind of religion in promoting community identity, popular performing arts and local solidarity.

Formal religions were more the concern of the educated élite, although elements filtered down into the practices of the common people: Buddhism achieved a mass following at certain periods, and Taoism influenced popular cults. Buddhism was introduced into China in the early centuries AD, having originated in India in the fifth century BC. It was at first mostly confined to foreign residents, but under the Eastern Chin (fifth century AD) began to spread among native Chinese. The following centuries saw a rapid expansion of Buddhism which reached its peak in the Tang dynasty (seventh to ninth centuries). The most popular sects were the Pure Land and the Chan, the latter being well known in the West via its Japanese derivative Zen. It is difficult to summarize the range of doctrines preached by different schools, but most of them advocated compassion, piety and devotion to the Buddha. Buddhism never fully recovered from a severe persecution in the ninth century, but it still remained an integral part of the Chinese religious scene. Hundreds of monasteries remained open until the

Cultural Revolution, and many of them re-opened in the 1980s. Buddhist philosophy exerted a profound influence over the culture of the élite as can be seen in the famous classical poetry of the Tang dynasty. A certain sense of fatalism and a longing for the quietness of monastic life, for example, are poetic themes which can be traced, at least in part, to Buddhism.

Taoism is a term applied to the philosophy attributed to two figures of uncertain historicity, Lao Zi and Zhuang Zi, who asserted the existence of an unseen, inexpressible Absolute, known as the Tao, pervading the universe. Their works, dating from about the third century BC, discuss how a person could become a sage by following the Tao, abandoning worldly desires and acting spontaneously. Taoism later evolved an esoteric system of religious beliefs centred on the achievement of immortality. This quest was pursued by a variety of occult means including alchemy, rituals, exercises akin to yoga, and chanting scriptures. The poem attributed to Lao Zi, the *Tao Te Ching*, is one of the most celebrated works of Chinese spirituality, containing famous lines such as 'Those who know do not speak; those who speak do not know' and 'The further one travels the less one knows. Therefore the Sage arrives without going, sees all without looking, does nothing yet achieves everything'. If the typical Buddhist figure is the pious monk, the Taoist is the hermit. Taoism was regarded by many of the élite as an alternative to the conventional state philosophy of Confucianism. Scholars who became disillusioned with the life of the court had the option of wandering away from the mundane world. There are many accounts of such men who retired to remote rural areas where they devoted themselves to meditation, the study of the yin and yang of nature, medicinal herbs, music or poetry. These sages, it was thought, could attain the blessed state of immortality. Whether or not anyone was successful in this enterprise, it became an essential element of Chinese culture which exerted a fascination for generations of Chinese scholars.

Confucianism could be considered a philosophy rather than a religion, but in either case is central to any consideration of the Chinese world-view. Originally the teachings of Confucius (*c.* 550–480 BC) focused on humanistic ethics and moral conduct. He dismissed speculation about the supernatural and insisted on the need for personal responsibility in the context of formal relationships between men and women, parents and children, rulers and subjects. In later centuries Confucianism was adopted as the state orthodoxy and came to dominate official thinking, culture and education. Its political expression was the veneration of the emperor as supreme ruler by virtue of a heavenly mandate and the creation of an elaborate ritual around him. The imperial system was totally discredited and overthrown in the twentieth century but as the dominant ideology of the scholar-official class Confucianism exerted enormous influence on the Chinese consciousness.

Finally, Islam was taken to China in the eighth century by Arab and Persian merchants. By the sixteenth century many Muslims were integrated into Chinese society, although in the nineteenth century, under the influence of the Naqshbandi Sufi Order, there were fierce Muslim revolts in outlying provinces. Apart from about 20 million Sinified and integrated Chinese Muslims, there are today important minorities in Xinjiang, Ningxia, Gansu and Yunnan provinces, totalling perhaps 15 million.

As will be apparent from this brief survey, religion in China was generally far more diffuse than in the European traditions. Many people combined elements of different beliefs in a personal synthesis, and there was no arbiter of orthodoxy to criticize them provided that they did not offend the state. More typical than devout belief in a particular religion, as far as the culture of the élite itself was concerned, was a kind of spirituality, strongly influenced by religious insights and values, expressed in music, painting and poetry. From the earliest written records, Chinese poetry was deeply concerned with the juxtaposition of the human and the natural world. In both painting and poetry this theme was taken up by the most famous artists in every generation, just as Christian themes were in the history of Western art.

In the post-1949 period state policy had a strong impact on Chinese religious life. The Chinese Communist Party (CCP) generally adopted a Leninist anti-religious stance in which 'religion' was seen as superstitious, unscientific, an opium of the people, a tool used by reactionary classes to confuse the oppressed, an ideological justification for preserving social inequality. The theory maintains that religion will die out in socialist society — a prediction which, so far at least, has not been fulfilled.

Practical measures adopted by the CCP have varied at different times since 1949 from extreme repression ('leftism') to acceptance in the interests of United Front work (in 'liberal' phases). The 'leftist' line aims to speed up the process of eradication by active persecution, while 'liberal' policies lay emphasis on obtaining believers' co-operation with government authority, to promote national unity and reconstruction.

Even in liberal times, however, there has been a tendency for religious belief to be discouraged by education campaigns, police surveillance and other forms of harassment. A factor which has important implications for religious policy is the international connections of religious organizations. Islamic, Buddhist and Christian groups have links with influential organizations in the Middle East, Japan, the USA and elsewhere, and religious grievances in China would risk alienating opinion in those countries. However, such connections can also lead to accusations of crypto-imperialism; Christians in particular have sometimes been fiercely criticized for their alleged links with the West.

In the early 1950s, the United Front Work Department, a CCP organ for liaison with non-Communist groups such as overseas Chinese and national minorities, set up the Religious Affairs Bureau under the State Council to implement CCP policy with respect to religious believers. Religious groups were instructed to organize 'Patriotic Associations' to liaise with officialdom, receive government orders and report on their own activities. Organizations and individuals who refused to participate in these schemes often faced persecution. Government control of religions after 1949 bore striking resemblances to the imperial system, which also tolerated state-registered heterodox organizations but suppressed illegal heterodoxies which were perceived as a challenge.

In the 1950s CCP policy with regard to Christians focused on two major issues: elimination of foreign influence and loyalty to the new government. This led to the mass expulsion of missionaries and the arrest of non-co-operative religious leaders. Two national Christian movements were founded, the Three Self Patriotic Movement (Protestant, TSPM) and the Chinese Patriotic Catholic Association (CPCA), which represent Christians legally and openly on the one hand, and are expected to relay government policy to believers on the other. In 1980 members of the TSPM founded the China Christian Council (CCC), with which it works closely: the TSPM represents the Church more in civil and political issues, the CCC has more ecclesiastical and pastoral responsibility. One of the most serious problems facing Chinese Christianity is the lack of trained leaders: many are elderly and there are far too few to provide adequate pastoral care. The TSPM/CCC now place great emphasis on training a new generation of Christian leaders through their seminaries and correspondence courses.

The TSPM/CCC are recognized by millions of believers, by the Chinese government and by many foreign Church bodies as the official representative of the Protestant Chinese Church. They have open churches, printing facilities and seminaries and their leaders are allowed to make frequent visits abroad. However, there are some critics who do not accept the TSPM as the true representative of Chinese Christianity, maintaining that its leaders are too subservient to the government. The tensions are most marked between the TSPM and evangelical groups which tend to exist on the borders of legality, leading a semi-clandestine existence constantly subject to harassment from government officials. For many Christians the alternative to TSPM church services has been small meetings held in believers' homes (sometimes known as the 'house church movement') which have been reported in enthusiastic, perhaps over-romanticized terms.

Here we can only point to a dilemma which has been faced by religious believers and leaders in other countries with anti-religious orthodoxies. Some may take a purist stand and resolutely oppose co-operation with governmental authority, sometimes courting repression and imprisonment. Others, such as the TSPM leaders, work within the state framework, accepting compromises and trying to negotiate a legal status for their activities. This is the strategy adopted by, for example, Bishop K. H. Ting, who has emerged as the leading figure of the TSPM/CCC.

The Catholic Church also has internal tensions. Because of CCP policy and the serious diplomatic rift between Beijing and the Vatican, Chinese Catholics were obliged either to reject papal authority and to join the CPCA or to adopt the alternative of becoming a catacomb Church with a precarious existence. This led them to adopt an interesting ecclesiology, maintaining that obedience to the Pope and acceptance of the Vatican's right to appoint bishops are not essential parts of Catholicism. The CPCA and its sister organizations accept some kind of spiritual affinity with the international Catholic Church; but politically they support government policy and insist on full independence from Rome. This has understandably led to chilly relations between the CPCA and the Vatican. Some Chinese Catholics have refused to co-operate with the official organizations and maintain clandestine links with Rome.

There may of course be many reasons why Christians join different associations. For example, some Catholics might pay lip-service to the CPCA and make use of its facilities while retaining personal feelings of loyalty to the Vatican; others might join an 'unofficial' evangelical sect simply because the official Church is not active in their district; leaders may genuinely subscribe to government policies or may do so purely out of expediency. Undoubtedly tensions exist between different groupings, but there is a large grey area between the two extremes of enthusiastic government support and outright opposition. It seems to us probable that very many believers simply want to join with other Christians in worship and prayer meetings, and are happiest when not obliged to adopt overt political stances — and perhaps this is not so different from the situation in most countries.

Estimates of the numbers of Christians in China are notoriously unreliable. However, there is evidence that the numbers have increased dramatically in the last decade, and that Christians now form an influential, numerically significant minority in some provinces and cities. Official sources (including the TSPM) tend to favour more conservative estimates, while some evangelical sources tend to exaggeration — thus one can find estimates ranging from a scant 5 million to an over-optimistic 100 million. A reasonable estimate might be around 20 million Protestants, of whom the majority would be only loosely associated with the TSPM, and perhaps 5 million Catholics. Catholics appear to have the slower growth rate, but it may also be that their communities are more cohesive and will be less subject to fluctuation in case of renewed political repression. The total figure represents only about 2.5 per cent of China's population, but the proportion is much higher in cities such as Kaifeng, Wenzhou, Xiamen, Fuzhou and surrounding rural areas. The proportion of Christians is usually highest where missionary activity was strongest.

The liberal 1980s were on the whole a period of growth for religions in China. Buddhism, Taoism and popular religions all experienced a resurgence of interest and enthusiasm. It seems that among the peasant population and even among intellectuals and students in the cities, people are seeking out temples and monasteries, organizing pilgrimages, attending services. The picture of Christianity in China today is of a varied, vibrant faith. Its adherents are spread throughout China, although thinly in many areas, facing political difficulties but not insurmountable ones. The situation is certainly far better than the most optimistic observer could have hoped for in the dark days of the Cultural Revolution. The future is unclear, and there are many sensitive issues to be resolved, yet on the whole believers must feel a certain confidence, having attained so much in an environment that appeared so unpromising. Moreover, Christianity has put down deep roots among Chinese communities in Hong Kong, Taiwan, Singapore and elsewhere.

The passages in this book shed some light on the history of Christianity in China, and they also show an impressive variety and depth of spirituality. In a Christian context spirituality is the inner pilgrimage which a Christian undertakes on earth, a pilgrimage of faith where Christians experience a living God within their concrete reality. The experience in faith may vary depending on social, cultural and historical contexts, but centres on the very same living

God who is universal to all. Chinese Christians live in a unique context and manifest a rather distinctive type of Christian spirituality, yet this spirituality may find resonance in other parts of Christendom.

Because of its unique context, the spiritual pilgrimage of Christians in China seems to have several distinctive characteristics which we have used to determine the sections of this book: perseverance in suffering, moral conduct, Christocentric devotion, nationalism, cultural continuity and evangelism. It is worth considering these in turn.

Ever since the seventh century, Christians have faced various degrees of persecution. Even in contemporary China, Christians have suffered discrimination and suppression. Since 1949 they have been victims of numerous political campaigns, particularly in the Cultural Revolution (1966–76) when believers were arrested, jailed, sent to hard labour camps, tortured and even killed for their faith. Nevertheless the Christian community has not diminished but rather increased many times over. And in response to the hostile environment, it has developed a unique spirituality of perseverance, with eschatological hope as its desire and the Cross as its glory. It draws strength from its powerlessness, to witness to the living God in an atheistic climate.

Chinese Christians also strongly emphasize correct moral conduct, as can be seen for example in the writing of Wang Mingdao or folk hymns from rural areas. Probably this characteristic is not an expression of Christian legalism so much as of Confucian ethics which, in theory at least, pervaded traditional Chinese culture. Confucianism stressed the supreme importance of correct conduct in various social relationships, and it is interesting to observe the preservation and transformation of this idea when adopted by Chinese Christians.

Another characteristic is the emphasis on Christ. Christocentric spirituality can be found in almost all Chinese devotional material. However it does not seem to be so much modelling oneself on the personality of Christ which appeals to Chinese Christians, but rather the desire to undergo a deep and mystical union with him. They long for the consolation of this mystical union, particularly in times of hardship, and it is perhaps this sense of personal identification which gives them the strength to endure the many trials and sufferings imposed on them.

A major factor in producing anti-Christian feelings in China has been the humiliation China has suffered at the hands of Western powers in the past 150 years. Chinese Christians have often highlighted their fervent nationalism and patriotism in an attempt to dissociate themselves from foreign power. Their active faith in an independent Chinese nation can be seen not only in words but in deeds, for example participation in economic reconstruction, assertion of national identity and active evangelism among compatriots. In particular the 1920s and 1930s witnessed the formation of many indigenous Chinese churches which emphasized their independence and declined assistance from foreign missionaries.

Another feature of Chinese Christian spirituality is the expression of faith in literary form, particularly poetry. An appealing aspect of Chinese classical poetry is its ability to convey the free spirit of Taoism, often placing creatures in the context of the beauty of nature. Those Chinese Christians who are well versed in the Chinese classics find classical poetry a means to merge some of the atmosphere of Taoism with the beauty of creation in the Christian tradition. Although some of the subtle beauties of poetry are inevitably lost in translation one can still appreciate this marriage between Taoism and Christianity.

Finally we should note an emphasis on evangelism: personal salvation through the acceptance of Jesus Christ as Saviour, and dedication to spreading the Gospel. The zealous desire for evangelism is perhaps a continuation of the enthusiasm of the missionaries who came to China during the past century. Evangelism was the primary objective of most missionaries and therefore of many of the Chinese leaders trained by them. This spirit of evangelism has called many Chinese Christians to pay a high price, sometimes even sacrificing their lives, in order to spread the Good News to places previously without any Christian presence.

Although the Christian community in China has always been relatively small numerically in proportion to China's population, it has had an undue influence. One can observe that the Christian spirit, symbols and ideas have permeated various strata in Chinese society. For example the democratic movement of university students in 1989 adopted several Christian symbols and concepts which had not previously been an element in Chinese discourse. Hunger-strikers on Tiananmen Square asserted that human rights are given by God — and one should remember that their school education was entirely atheist. When protesters erected the statue of the Goddess of Democracy, they sang not the 'Internationale' but a Christian hymn: 'Joyful Joyful We Adore Thee'. Some students who escaped the massacre wrote to others to 'pray for those who died so that they may rest with God in Heaven'.

Christian spirituality in China has in the past generally been concerned with issues such as grace, salvation, repentance and devotion. Perhaps it is now also beginning to find expression in the socio-political realm: as a source of inspiration for Chinese people searching for democracy and human dignity under a totalitarian regime. There is a complex relationship between Christianity, a great world religion, and China, an ancient civilization encompassing a quarter of the world's population. We hope that readers find in the selection of material some illumination of this great meeting of traditions, and also some pointers to universal themes of life and death, humanity and God.

SECTION ONE

Perseverance in Suffering

If other people do not cause me suffering, how can I grind down and smooth off my own rough edges?

Jin Danyin (1890–?1953), founder of Jesus Family, an indigenous movement which is characterized by a commune-like Christian community. The movement was started in Shandong province in the 1930s and still survives.

Christianity in China has had to survive in an often hostile environment. From the 1850s to 1949 there were frequent anti-Christian movements, sometimes supported by officials, and many Christians were persecuted because of their belief. After 1949 their difficulties increased because of the government's hostility to religion, and in some periods, for example the Cultural Revolution, believers constantly faced imprisonment or death. Chinese Christians have produced moving accounts of faith in times of suffering, showing how hardship can be transformed into spiritual insight.

Prayers and thoughts of Chinese Christians

1

The Final Farewell Blessing

Simon Zhao (?1925–), originally from Shenyang, felt a calling to undertake evangelistic work in the late 1940s. In 1949 he and his wife, along with two others, went to Xinjiang, a remote, undeveloped province in the far north-west of China. He was arrested in 1951 and suffered many hardships because of his faith. His wife died in prison in 1960, but Simon did not receive the news until 1973. He was released in the early 1980s and became a legend among the Christians of Xinjiang, where he is still an active pastor. He wrote many hymns and poems which became a source of encouragement and hope.

When I think of my own family separated for many years
My heart sheds drops of blood
My memory relives these painful moments
From the depth of my long frozen heart
That was the final farewell
Escorted by rifles, hands locked in chains
Between life and death
After several months of separation I saw my own house
Shrinking in a cold street,   on a gloomy corner
The investigators had once struck the plaintive, quiet, troubled
    door   which still shivers in misery and fear
Did anyone there know that their dear one was approaching
In a prison van, soundless
Then soundlessly leaving them
In this fleeting dreamlike moment?
Farewell
(I did not expect this was the final farewell)
How could I stop the wheels, the horses' hooves
To cast a final glance on my home
How could I break my handcuffs and leg-irons
Strain my voice   to cry at the door
To strengthen my brothers' determination:
'Do not fear   bloodshed and knives
Can engulf only our bodies
But they can never never shake
The eternal truth of the Cross'

Farewell
I did not know whether this separation would lead
To the ends of the earth or the place of skulls
But I had chosen the Cross, to follow
The footsteps of Jesus Christ stained with blood.

Farewell
I could only bear the heart-breaking agony
Silently pray for the peace of God's house
Wish that in the midst of adversity
God might stretch out his hand to protect his children from my
    fate:
Persecuted by others, contemptuously cast aside.
Thirty years have passed in a flash.

Did they know the blessing made in the prison van then?
I myself passed through the curse of death
Died and revived. Once more as if in a dream
I hear the cries of Abel
Come from blood under the sacrificial altar
Come from songs behind prison bars

As it turned out, among those I blessed from the prison van then
Some were also bound and put in jail
Where they drank the cup of bitterness to the last drop
The last witnesses had gone
No wreaths   no graves   no gravestones.
Nobody could find her body
No name was left behind
All that was left: the sweet fragrance of Jesus
Given from the Cross to every living person.

Today when I remember my family —
Separated for many years, my heart sheds tears of blood —
My faith revives in the midst of these painful moments

From the depth of my long frozen heart
See! The seeds of blood under the sacrificial altar
Will bear fruit, becoming countless immortal lives
Bursting through harsh winter
Bursting through dark night
Bursting through the shackles of death.

2

An anonymous hymn written at the height of the Cultural Revolution.

> The will of God is mysterious, hard to fathom,
> So everything depends on oneself
> I firmly believe God's intentions are perfect
> Full of grace and kindness.
>
> The diseases and miseries we have suffered
> Are expressions of the Lord's love
> Everything in the world interacts
> So we have benefited from all our sufferings.*
>
> Sometimes we feel distressed and pained
> We do not know the Lord's will
> But we know our Lord is never mistaken
> So we should still trust and obey him.
>
> I am the clay, the Lord is the potter
> He lays his affection and strength on me
> With good intentions and masterly skill
> The Lord fashions a valuable vessel.
>
> Only if we obey to the end can we know God's will
> So good, kind and mysterious
> There is sweetness in the bitter, kindness in the severe
> The Lord attains his purpose through his love.
>
> Chorus:
> The Lord's will is mysterious
> The Lord's will is hard to fathom
> His will is full of grace and kindness
> It fills me with great comfort.

---

* A reference to the passage in Romans 8.28, 'In all things God works for the benefit of his people'. The concept of universal interaction is deeply rooted in Chinese philosophy.

3

Song of Praise from the Soul

The author of this hymn is a physician. Because of her Christian faith she was separated from her family and worked alone in North China for 21 years. She survived an earthquake and car accidents. She left China in the early 1980s.

> I look back on the mercy and love of the Lord
> In his mercy he cared for me.
> One can truly never describe the Lord's love
> The mercies of the Lord can never be counted.
>
> In sickness the Lord was the doctor who healed
> In earthquake and accidents he saved.
> He calmed the wild winds and fierce seas
> Now is the moment of Emmanuel.
>
> Now I offer my heart to the Father
> I will be a steadfast worker for the Lord.
> My hands will diligently work for the Lord
> My feet will follow closely in his footsteps.
>
> Life on earth is short and in vain
> Heaven is my new home for eternity.
> Watchfully awaiting the second coming of the Lord
> This is my heart's beloved desire.
>
> My heart magnifies the Lord
> My soul rejoices in God
> Hosanna! Glory be to God
> Hallelujah! Praise the Lord.

4

By Wang Mingdao (1900–), one of the most famous of Chinese Christian preachers. An independent pastor and prolific writer, he established the Beijing Christian Tabernacle in 1924 and published his own journal entitled Spiritual Food Quarterly.

He became known as a 'man of iron' for his refusal to compromise with the secular authorities, which resulted in 25 years' imprisonment from 1955 to 1980. He is a deeply respected figure and has become a living symbol of faith for many Chinese Christians.

Even in the troubled days of our life we should still praise him.
Thank the Lord for saving us, for calling us.
Thank the Lord that in the midst of difficult times we are still alive.
Thank the Lord for bestowing upon us all kinds of spiritual blessings.
Thank the Lord for bestowing upon us hope and trust in him.
Thank the Lord for bestowing upon us comfort and joy.
Thank the Lord for bestowing upon us the strength to endure hardship.
Thank the Lord that he has not treated us according to our sins.
Thank the Lord for his promise to bestow on us a heavenly eternal home, a kingdom that can never be shaken, and incomparable, everlasting glory.

Be thankful that by the grace of our Lord Jesus we can go calmly and without fear into the Presence of God, we can receive forgiveness and the blessing of his mercy, his help and protection at all times.

If we have truly learned to 'give thanks in all circumstances' then even in times of trouble we will never feel the slightest hardship.

5

The Rev. Dr Francis Xavier Chu Shih-de SJ received his doctorate in France. He returned to China, was jailed in 1953 and died in jail in 1983. He wrote this letter to his brother in 1949 before boarding the plane for Shanghai.

Every day many people are escaping from China to Hong Kong. Yet I cannot find any one, apart from myself, who is preparing to leave Hong Kong for China. Everyone laughs at me for being a fool. In the eyes of the world I am indeed the biggest fool ever born! When a merchant cannot make a profit in one place, he will move somewhere else. Yet I am a priest, and the life of a priest is to serve his flock. As long as there are Christians left in Shanghai, I must return there. Even if there is not a single Christian left in Shanghai, I must still return there. Because I am a priest. I represent Christ and his Church. Wherever I am, the Church is. I am willing to stay in Shanghai, to let the Communist Party know that the Catholic faith is still alive.

6

Written by a Christian woman, imprisoned for over twenty years from the 1950s. Wishing to remain anonymous she used the pseudonym 'Little Dust' for a devotional booklet she wrote, probably while she was in jail. The manuscript was circulated in handwritten form among Christians in China and later published in Hong Kong.

Dear brothers and sisters, we are sometimes beset by hardships. Things seem more evil every day, our situation becomes ever worse, the night is so dark that we cannot even see our hands in front of our faces. Now is the time we must learn from Job, to go into the presence of our Lord, to stand before his countenance and to comprehend his will. Since we know 'this too comes from God' then we will humbly accept and obey, safe in the Lord's hands. For God is master of every situation. Nothing we encounter is a coincidence. Everything is assuredly in God's beautiful plan. He does not call us to suffer in vain. He is the Eternal and Almighty One. He calls us to traverse fire and water but we will reach the promised land. He leads us to walk the road of the Cross because this road leads straight to his glorious throne.

7

Explanation without Words

Another poem by Simon Zhao (see no. 1), written on learning of his wife's death in prison.

Some people
To evaluate the life   of a dead person
As a yard-stick   use social effect
(i.e. what and   how much that person
contributed to society)

Some people
To evaluate the life   of a dead person
As a yard-stick   use the beauty of a garland
(i.e. the magnificent   but spurious things
associated with the dead person)

Other people
To evaluate the life   of a dead person
As a yard-stick   use sunglasses
(i.e. everything   is black
associated with the dead person)

She alone used her own blood
Explained without words that
To evaluate the life of a dead person
As a yard-stick   use the dead person's blood

(but as for her blood, nobody cared to look)
Although she was part of the world
She did not belong to the world
Her body was abandoned at an unmarked burial ground
Her corpse bore witness to the Lord
The theoretical logic of this world
Also left her far away   far away

Ah   eyes attached to this world —
How can they recognize footprints of heaven
When the love of God   sacrificed on the cross
Consumed her like fire
In the midst of fire   from the altar of sacrifice

She followed the Lord
Left her family and home,
Passed through the smoke of cannons
Crossed the Yangtze   and Yellow River
Pursued to wilderness desert sands . . .

To spread the message of the Cross and the Lord who died for us
She went to that ancient city — ghost-haunted
Ah — but that city
Opened its mouth and swallowed her blood.

8

By Archbishop Dominic Deng Yiming SJ, of Guangzhou. He has been the Apostolic Administrator of Guangzhou (Canton) since 1951. He was arrested in 1958, sent to labour camps, and released in 1980, when he went to Hong Kong for medical treatment. Since being consecrated Archbishop by the Holy See in 1981 he has remained in exile in Hong Kong.

Every day I prayed, meditated and sang hymns so that I had no free time. These spiritual exercises were the same every day and supported me for the long years of prison life and gave me strength to overcome both material and spiritual hardships and to have a serene heart. God gave me the grace of an optimistic spirit, encouraging me to look constantly at the good side of things and seldom at the bad side. I was imprisoned for God, for the Church; my conscience was at peace, as I had done my duty towards God and the Church. If I were to die some day I would die in peace. If I were released I would continue to serve God and the Church. These happy thoughts and feelings, this peace in the depth of my soul, supported my spirit during the 22 long winters and summers of my prison life.

9

Bitter Cup

A hymn written in 1983 by Simon Zhao (see no. 1) which many Chinese Christians find a powerful expression of the years of suffering they have undergone.

Bitter cup, bitter cup,
The bitter cup of the Lord which is hard to drink
Silently obeying the Heavenly Father
Bitterness enters the bone.

In Gethsemane he sweated as if bleeding — for whom?
He bore the pain of whipping — for whom?

He went to death, Cross on back — for whom?
He was butchered like a lamb, without a cry — for whom?

He was deserted by God's people and nailed on the Cross — for whom?
In obedience he shed his last drop of blood — for whom?

Chorus:
Bitter cup, bitter cup — for me! for me!

10

Another poem by Simon Zhao (see no. 1). After his release from prison in 1980 he searched for Christian fellowship but failed to find any. The song is an expression of his loneliness and desolation at that time.

> So many years of wailing winds and bitter rain,
> So many years of violent storms
> Unseen in the tempest is the courtyard of the Lord
> Shed on the sacrificial altar is the fresh blood of Abraham
> Where are you, vine of God?
> Where are you, fragrant pine tree of God?
> Where are you? Where are you?

Every lamb is crying out, every lost sheep is sorrowing
The sheep of Jehovah are astray on the steppes
The tears of the distressed are shed in the west wind.
Where are you, good Shepherd?
Where are you, good Protector?
Where are you? Where are you?

Jerusalem in my dreams, Jerusalem in my tears.
I have sought you in the fire of the sacrificial altar
I have sought you in the nail holes of the Cross
How long before I can leave the Valley of Tears?
How long before I can return to home in paradise?
How long? How long?

11

The Place of Skulls

This hymn was written in the early 1980s after the author had witnessed the martyrdom of some of his colleagues.

In the depths of history, in remote clouds and mountains
Lies silently sleeping a desolate land
The Cross has long been lost
The precious blood long forgotten
Who recalls those pain filled cries?
Who knows from where the Gospel that we hear today
Was preached in the past?
The gate to Heaven was opened here
The power of sin started to collapse here.

Mortal beings perished here, Adam was buried here
Sorrows and tears have all passed away
Satan feels ashamed here
The Cross is shining here
The word of God is proclaimed.
Let us hurry to preach the Gospel far and wide
Let us sound the trumpet, hesitate no more.
Look! The Mount of Olives has burst open
Long cherished sunlight of morning is just appearing.

12

Written in 1973, at the height of the Cultural Revolution when all churches were closed, many were destroyed and the persecution of religious believers was most severe. It was the context of darkness and seeming hopelessness which inspired this hymn.

If I am to suffer, if it is for the Lord
My heart will be full of joy, full of joy
I urge the Holy Spirit to hold me on a tight rein
I beg the Holy Spirit to purify my words, deeds and thoughts
Thus I prepare to meet the Lord should I die.

My sufferings were not too long or hard
But they bring unparalleled great glory
If my honour is compared to the humiliations
Contempt, curses and death are of no consequence.

We were fortunate to have the prophets like beacons in the dark
The harder the circumstances, the brighter my soul
I beg the Lord for strength to survive a while longer
The one who comes will redress injustice for the innocent.

I should follow the Lord with firm belief
I should bear fruit every day
I should rid myself of sinful thoughts
I should ignore the influence of other people and circumstances
Only seek the favour of the Lord
To take me to Paradise when I die.

Fellow Christians are separated by thousands of miles and
 mountain ranges
Separated in body, but we meet in spirit
When the last trumpet is sounded, in an instant
Saints from all times and all places will meet together and never
 part.

13

Song of Remembrance

Yu Yang, a Christian leader in China, wrote this poem in the late 1970s, dedicated to those Christians who suffered persecution by the authorities.

You sympathize with those families who were persecuted;
by the Grace of God you share with them what you have earned
  through your hard labour, you offer them money and food.

You care for the abandoned widows and orphans;
with the love of Christ and a devoted spirit you relieve their
  afflictions and tend their wounds.

You stir up the flame of love in the hearts of our sisters;
so that in the stormy winter nights they can care for each other,
  warm each other and be faithful.

You strengthen the brothers' faith in Christ;
in order that they can firmly uphold the Truth without yielding
  and sing hymns even on a dark silent night.

My dear brother it is you
Following the example of our good Shepherd
Who bravely protects the flock of God.
It is you who willingly offers
The alabaster jar of perfume,*
An expression of your love for Jesus.

*Reference to Mark 14.3–9.

14

The suppression of the student democracy movement on 4 June 1989 made a profound impact in many sections of Chinese society. This letter was written by a group of Christian students in Jinan University to Samuel Lam (Lin Xiangao), pastor of a well-known house church in Guangzhou. The church was threatened with closure by the authorities as part of the crackdown after 4 June.

Paul's misfortunes are a constant reminder to us that we should be fully prepared to suffer for the Lord at any time. And his words are even more moving. We seem to be dying, but in fact we are alive. We seem to be punished, but we will not lose life. We seem to be sad, but we are always rejoicing. We seem to be poor, but we make many others rich. We seem to own nothing, but actually have everything. In Psalm 73, the psalmist is not just describing the situation of that time: is it not like the world today also? We feel upset when vicious people arrogantly enjoy a secure life. They mock others, they speak evil words to bully others. They are arrogant and conceited. They blaspheme Heaven and slander the earth. However, when the psalmist entered the Holy Temple and pondered over their final fate, his mind changed completely and he was filled with hope from God.

SECTION TWO

Moral Conduct

Christianity uses the moral integrity taught by Christ to save the nation. The moral integrity taught by Christ is characterized by loyalty, honesty, benevolence, righteousness, unselfishness, modesty, faithfulness, co-operation, friendliness, responsibility, dedication, will-power. Christians will never despair but will struggle to the death for the nation and for justice.

Jian Youwen, a Christian leader in the 1920s.

The cultivation of moral qualities has been a central theme in Chinese philosophy for over 2,000 years. The Confucian tradition in particular stressed the importance of correct behaviour in relationships with other human beings. Christian moral teachings are therefore relatively familar and acceptable to people brought up in China and form an important element of the Christian tradition there.

15

This and nos 16 to 18 are typical of the moral writings of Wang Mingdao (see no. 4).

Do not trust people nor doubt people easily.
Do not casually judge someone as good or bad unless the evidence is crystal clear.
Do not judge anyone lightly — not by words, nor even in the heart.
A prejudiced person is like someone wearing tinted spectacles — everything seen bears a tinted colour.
It is a great sin to think evil of others: it may easily cause not only injustice and harm to others but also serious damage to oneself.
Laughing at someone's shortcomings is extremely ignorant and harmful.
To benefit others is your duty, to accept gifts from others is to receive grace.
Never remember your goodness when you help others; never forget their goodness when others help you.
Only a wise person can see the goodness in enemies and recognize the weakness of loved ones.

16

God often makes hardships turn to our profit. When we have understood this, we can easily praise God for our sufferings.

Hardships bring to light and even dispel many sins hidden in our hearts. They cause us to abandon arrogance and self-satisfaction, destroy the power that the world has over us, make us detached from worldly riches, focus us on the wealth of the spirit, make us believe and rely entirely on God.

At these times God seems to say: 'I am now testing you, to see if you can trust me to the end, is your faith sufficient for this?'

Suffering hones our whole personality to make it beautiful and complete, makes us gentle and fresh, more patient, richer in sympathy, more completely loving. Suffering makes us understand anew how God's mercy and wisdom have the power to fulfil our needs.

This understanding is the highest blessing, sufficient to compensate for the pains we suffer — more than sufficient.

17

Unless a person can categorically lay aside money, reputation and life, he cannot become very strong. Thank God that in the past decades I was able to put aside money and reputation. The only thing that I could not disregard was the critical issue of life and death. In 1955 I met with extremely terrible circumstances which made me weak for ten years.

Today I have stood up straight, thrown aside my weakness, and nothing more can frighten me! Because our Lord has already triumphed over death, thank God, I can praise victory in Christ.

18

Today the majority of churches have fallen into a very pitiful condition. Many resplendent and magnificent, beautiful and ornate churches are like this. Inside they have fine fittings, comfortable seats, melodious instruments, harmonious choirs, copper crucifixes and snow-white candles. The priest wears formal black robes, a beautiful sash at his waist, reads from a de luxe edition prayer book and preaches an impeccable sermon. The congregation stands respectfully to sing hymns, sits quietly to hear the sermon and stretches out to put money in the collection boxes.

Seen from the eyes of God, this is like an egg-shell that lacks both yolk and egg-white.

There are people who like to eat raw eggs. They make a small hole at each end of the shell with a needle, leave one hole open and suck sharply through the other hole until the white and the yolk have both been drawn out. Then they put the empty shell back in the tray. From the outside it still looks like a whole egg, but in fact there is only a useless shell left.

Today many churches in the world are like this. Only the eyes of God and the eyes of those who understand God's will can see the emptiness of today's churches.

The churches are only external things, but the holiness, justice, honesty, love, faith and hope that God wants from the church have all long been bankrupt.

19

A hymn sung by Christian communities in rural areas of Anhui province. It is interesting to see how this and several other pieces refer to relationships in the extended family, which still form the basic social structure for most Chinese people. Particularly in rural society, a new wife becomes an integral part of her husband's family and is expected to obey her parents-in-law. The relationship between daughter-in-law and mother-in-law is of central importance to family life, and also a common source of family discord. Hence the exhortations to all parties to exercise restraint and display considerate behaviour.

I urge people to practise filial piety, because our parents' great kindness is hard to repay. Children pass faeces and urine, and who else cares if they sleep in a wet bed or a dry one?

When a son is taken ill, his mother will be very anxious. She will not eat or sleep, praying for her son day and night. If he often becomes ill, she will break her heart with worry.

When the boy is four or five years old she no longer has to hold him in her arms but he is always shouting and crying. She fears he will go swimming in the river or climbing trees after birds.

When the son is fifteen or sixteen he begins to understand things but he often behaves rudely to his family. He shows no respect for his elders and does not care for the young. He forgets his parents' great kindness.

When he gets married he will save money for his own family and again forget about his parents.

When he has a son of his own he will hold him in his arms. His son has beautiful clothes and fancy hats to wear, and he calls him pretty names as they walk along the road.

Since you know how to love your children, how can you forget your parents' love for you? Water from a bitter well is not sweet, brambles cannot bear grapes, thorns cannot produce grain. Good will reap good, evil will reap evil. One generation succeeds another along life's road. An unfilial child will have an unfilial child of his own.

I urge the father- and mother-in-law to listen carefully. You should not quarrel with your daughter-in-law. It is she who does all the heavy housework, grinding the wheat and making noodles, husking rice and washing clothes.

She cooks three meals a day and boils the water, lighting the kitchen stove each time. Then she is busy late into the night, spinning, weaving, patching and knitting.

When you hand out food and clothes you should treat her fairly. God will be pleased if you love your daughter-in-law.

I urge the daughter-in-law to listen carefully. You should not quarrel with your father- and mother-in-law. They are old, they cannot do heavy work or move around easily. You should serve meals and wait on them. Try your best to show filial obedience to your parents-in-law.

The true God will help you to enjoy a long and happy life and you will have a daughter-in-law as filial as yourself. You will enjoy the reputation of being a pious daughter-in-law.

20

This extract is from a book entitled Living Water, *written by a preacher from Shandong, Zhang Jiakun. She was in prison from the 1950s until the 1970s but is now leading an active life as a pastor.* Living Water *was a devotional work written in the 1940s.*

From afar you see a high mountain and wonder how you can ever cross it. But however high the mountain is, you can always find a pathway over it.

At times our difficulties rise up in front of us like great mountains, and how can we pass over them? As long as we do not fear hardship, but walk onwards, a day will surely come when we have overcome them. External barriers cannot block our way forward, it is only despair and weakness in our spirit that can make us falter on the road.

In many cases it is not that the difficulties are insurmountable, but that our own self-imposed limitations make things difficult.

The Lord Jesus has already broken through all the barriers ahead of us. As long as we agree to go forward we can assuredly pass through.

SECTION THREE

Christocentric Devotion

> The LIFE given you by God
> is not an independent LIFE
>   this LIFE very naturally pushes you to
>   approach other similar LIFE forms . . .
> to share feelings, intimate feelings, with other LIFE.

Watchman Nee (see no. 22).

The characteristic expression of Chinese Christian spirituality is Christocentric devotion. Many preachers and writers have expressed an intense personal connection with Christ as father, protector, saviour and friend. We also find, although less often, deeply-felt personal prayers to God the Father and the Virgin Mary.

21

Dr John Sung (1901–44). Dr Sung was born into a Christian family in the province of Fujian. He completed a doctorate in chemistry in the United States, where he also studied theology. On his return journey he threw his diplomas overboard into the sea and determined to dedicate his life to preaching the Gospel. He led many revival meetings all over China and in South East Asia, and became perhaps the most successful evangelist of his time.

I have to recognize that there is a living force in the Bible, since whenever I have committed any sin in thought or word — those which I used not to count as sins, but which now, after my rebirth, I regard as serious — and I go to read the Bible, then the Bible criticizes my faults.

In every book, every chapter I always see the word 'sin' until I run before his throne of mercy and sincerely pray for forgiveness. After that, whenever I open the Bible at any point I find words of comfort from God, sentences full of riches and promises of the forgiveness of sins.

Or whenever I give rise to sly thoughts of admiration for worldly ways, the Bible's teaching is to despise the ways of the world. How could this be an ordinary kind of book? Praise God! The Word of the Lord is a bright lamp before my feet, light on the path.

I will hold the Lord's Word forever in my heart, since it is not only the food of my life but it keeps me from sin.

22

Watchman Nee (1906–72), an influential and controversial leader who, without any formal theological training, established the Little Flock movement which became the largest indigenous Christian group in the Chinese Church. He wrote many devotional books and his works were translated into several languages. He was arrested in the 1950s and died in prison.

Our life is the life of Christ entering into our life through the indwelling spirit. At the same time, the law of our life is natural. Once we have realized this reality we have to stop our struggles and cast aside our hypocrisy.

Nothing can cause more damage to Christian life than pretence. Nothing can be more blessed than stopping our external efforts and living out our natural being. Then our speech, prayer and life become a natural flow of our inner life.

Have we discovered the goodness of our Lord? When he is in us there is this kind of goodness. How great is his might? His might is not diminished even when he is in us.

Praise God, his life is eternally great. For those who dare to believe in his Word, this holy life will be manifested in power no less than in ancient times.

23

Watchman Nee.

I remember one morning sitting at a table upstairs, reading scriptures and praying, I said 'O Lord, open my eyes'. In an instant I saw.

I saw myself united with Christ, I saw myself inside him. When he died, I died. I saw that my death was a thing of the past, not a thing of the future. My death was as real as his, because when he died I was inside him. The whole question was thus illuminated for me.

The joy I received from this discovery was almost unbearable. I jumped up from the chair and called out in a loud voice: 'Praise the Lord I am dead!'

From that day until now, I have never had the least doubt about the definition of the phrase: 'I am already crucified with Christ'.

24

This and nos 25 to 27 are unusual examples of hymns from a rural area of China, Wuyang county in Henan province. They were collected by staff of the Hong Kong-based journal Bridge, *which regularly reports on church life in China. The simple, rhythmic style owes much to local folk traditions and will perhaps remind readers of spirituals from the southern USA.*

Old Granny believes in the Lord, she removes idols and respects the true God. She offers her rice-bowl to thank God and the Heavenly Father gives us a happy household. Peace and joy fill our days, ever moving forward to follow the Lord.

Old Granny believes in the Lord, her temper is much improved. She treats her daughters and daughters-in-law even-handedly. People say she is impartial and the glorious light of the Lord shines on everybody.

Elder brother believes in the Lord, he doesn't smash pots and pans, doesn't curse the chickens and dogs, doesn't lose his temper any more. When people see him they praise him.

Old Auntie believes in the Lord, she loves her husband and respects her relatives. The Gospel educates people to spend their days in joy and peace.

Young women believe in the Lord, they are able, virtuous and diligent, when they see Auntie they are so affectionate, they make others envious.

Girls believe in the Lord, they don't want to play but practise needlework, they don't wander around the houses telling lies, everybody who sees them praises them.

Young men believe in the Lord, they don't idle and cause mischief, they don't loudly curse their neighbours, their friends and relatives all come to see them, they believe in Jesus and become good men.

Students believe in the Lord, they don't want to play around, bluff and cheat, they never steal. Ah, mother and father smile and laugh when they see them.

25

Spiritual kinsmen who sit in the Holy Temple, be patient and do not think of your homes! Listen to my song of 'Ten Fresh Flowers'. The ten fresh flowers are growing in the Spirit, everyone praises them:

One flower blooms anew: respect mother and father with true piety, God knows false emotion and hypocrisy, the true God does not like that kind of person.

The second flower blooms greatly: do not listen to outsiders, it brings no good to be fussy, bad people's families come to grief in the end.

The third flower blooms purple: do not covet others' property, be generous with offerings to the Lord, trust that happiness will be yours by and by.

The fourth flower blooms red: speak of the Heavenly Father, speak of the Holy Spirit, never say an angry word, a happy smile and open face will receive the Holy Spirit.

The fifth flower blooms in goodness: there is no need to show off your goodness, bear a heavy load on the path of the Gospel, people do not know but God does.

The sixth flower blooms so large: use your gains to help others, if you hurt others with cunning flowery words, God will be angry and punish you.

The seventh flower blooms in purity: lies and curses hurt others' hearts. If the true God knows about it you will be so ashamed you will lose all self-respect.

The eighth flower blooms eight ways: the filial daughter-in-law respects her parents, piously teaches them what God likes, a light shines as she walks along the road.

The ninth flower blooms in the wild: worldly people first care for food and clothes, if there is nothing to eat or drink they grumble as they go along.

The tenth flower blooms completely: do not get involved in others' quarrels, if you are hit bear with it, if you say too much everyone will be annoyed.

Prayers and thoughts of Chinese Christians

26

1. I say who will come first, who will answer me first?
Who heals the sick to show miracles, who heals the sick to show miracles?
You say who will come first, I will answer you first.
Lord Jesus heals the sick to show miracles, Lord Jesus heals the sick to show miracles.

2. I say who will come second, who will answer me second?
Who betrays the Lord and insults God, who sells the Lord and insults God?
You say who will come second, I will answer you second.
Judas sells the Lord and insults God, Judas sells the Lord and insults God.

3. I say who will come third, who will answer me third?
Who ascends living to heaven, who ascends living to heaven?
You say who will come third, I will answer you third.
Elijah ascends living to heaven, Elijah ascends living to heaven.

4. Who led the chosen people out of Egypt?
Old Moses led the chosen people out of Egypt.

5. Who fell into the fiery lake?
The rich old man fell into the fiery lake.

6. Who was saved from death?
Lazarus was saved from death.

7. Who was put in a furnace?
Three prophets were put in a furnace.

8. Who believed in God and left his family?
Elisha believed in God and left his family.

9. Who made the great ark?
Old Noah made the great ark.

10. Who was taken up to heaven?
Enoch was taken up to heaven.

27

1. Thank you heavenly Father, you wrote this Bible for me. I beg the Holy Spirit for help, open my mind, let me see things clearly, keep me from walking astray.

2. God loves people so much that he gave his only begotten son to us, so that all who believe in him will not perish but may have eternal life.

3. The Holy Spirit draws near and descends on me. Then we surely receive the power of God and become a witness to the Lord in Jerusalem, Judaea, Samaria and to the ends of the earth.

4. Jesus has come to give life to his sheep, to give a life more abundant. Jesus is a good shepherd, a good shepherd protecting his sheep, a good shepherd protecting his flock.

5. Only if we respect the true God can we receive the true Gospel. Do not worship false Gods, remove all idols. Put aside worldly habits, abandon sin. The Lord comes to bless the children of the heavenly kingdom.

6. The Lord was nailed on the cross to set me free, to die and be resurrected together with the Lord, to spend my life in Christ, to win victory with the cross and defeat evil.

7. The heavenly kingdom is at hand, the time has arrived, repent as soon as possible. The grace of Jesus is higher than the sky. The sins of believers are forgiven, we receive peace and joy. We are free and happy forever.

8. Sins are forgiven, sickness is healed. We should be thankful, pray constantly, understand the Gospel, realize the truth, rely on the Lord for everything. The grace of Jesus is higher than the sky. The sins of believers are forgiven, we receive peace and joy. We are free and happy forever.

9. The false Gods have gone, the true God has come, the whole family has great happiness. Realizing the way of heaven, walking

the way of heaven, as if our spirits were singing. The grace of Jesus is higher than the sky. The sins of believers are forgiven, we receive peace and joy. We are free and happy forever.

10. The mind's eye has been opened, the Holy Spirit has entered, the true light shines steady within. The Saviour leads the way, brightly leads the way, we can truly reach heaven. The grace of Jesus is higher than the sky, we receive peace and joy. We are free and happy forever.

28

This and no. 29 are taken from a collection of devotional material written by an anonymous house-church leader in the late 1970s.

'Love the Lord your God with all your heart, with all your soul, with all your mind and all your strength.' (Mark 12.30)

God is love, only love is union with God, only love fills God with joy. God is love and he also wishes to be loved, he wishes an exchange of love, he wishes the universe to be filled with love.

In his creation God cannot find love that could fulfil him, so he hopes to find it among those who belong to him. His love is expressed through creation and salvation, his only demand is that you love him. This is the first and the greatest of God's commandments to his chosen people. We love because God loves us first. If a person loves God, that person is known by God.

God examines people's hearts, whoever loves God is known by him. If our achievements have not been or could not be very remarkable, if we are not praised by others, it is not important. If we are forgotten or even trampled underfoot, seemingly useless to God, we should not despair.

We need pursue only one thing, to love God with all our heart, all our soul, all our strength — then our life in the world will not be in vain, we will not be unworthy of God's grace.

To love God is more noble and more sweet than any other thing, it is the greatest joy for God. Here you can find the wellspring of living water and return to the deep source of life.

Love of God does not mean that you have to do many things,

but rather that you see what God wants you to do. Those who love God do not have selfish desires, they only have God. Put oneself on the altar, let the fire of love burn without end.

29

'Record my lament; list my tears on your scroll — are they not in your record?' (Psalm 56.8)

The Lord is extremely solicitous towards his sons and daughters. He has even counted the hairs on our heads, so how much more does he care for greater issues? He never forgets us, any more than a mother caring for a suckling baby. He sees our tears as still more precious, he treasures them. He does not lightly call us to shed one tear — so why does he still call us to weep?

When a person's body is wounded it loses blood, when the soul is wounded it sheds tears.

If someone has not shed tears, it shows a heart as hard as steel. Some people also have an easy life with little hardship and so have no tears to shed.

However, if one has always laughed and never known tears, this is not at all a sign of God's blessing. Not to feel wounded in an evil world, to be happy when one ought to mourn, is most displeasing to God.

Only if worries, sorrows and tears make happy smiles turn to mourning, joy turn to sadness, will the painful wounds cause God to show his grace.

The tears of repentance are precious. God will collect them drop by drop.

Tears arise from hardship, and not from ordinary hardships, but those which pierce the heart — if there are no such tears, there is no liberation. So shedding tears has a very profound meaning.

Shedding tears makes a person understand the world, makes one examine one's conscience, makes one look up to heaven.

Truly, water can wash dirt from the body, but tears can wash dirt from the mind. Tears confuse physical sight but illuminate the spirit.

Tears are often a turning point in a person's life and God often has to make us pour forth many tears.

Job's tears were noticed by God, the Israelites wept in Babylon, but they passed through the valley of tears and turned the valley into fertile land. When tears scatter seed, a harvest will be reaped.

Even more precious are the common people's tears for God, tears for the work of the Lord. One day God will wipe them all dry.

30

By Rev. Dr T. C. Chao (1895–1979), a famous theologian, pastor, writer and educator. Dr Chao, educated in China and the United States, was elected one of the six presidents of the First Assembly of the World Council of Churches in Amsterdam, 1948. He later joined the Three Self Patriotic Movement.

Today human eyes cannot see him, but he still lives in our souls. Fellowship with him brings the experience of reconstruction of moral qualities, brings forth living forces. People who believe in him, in their hearts, in communion, receive witness to his presence in a process which seems invisible and impossible but is a factual reality. Oh Jesus, you do not need us to worship you as God.

Without you we cannot know God, the creator and protector of the universe. We are unworthy, we should always learn from you. With you we have life, without you we are like lost sheep which have gone astray.

We want you to be together with us, teacher, friend! We want to sing hymns of praise to you, offering our sincere love and respect.

31

Beloved Lord You Call Me Back

By Rev. John Su (?1920–), pastor, writer, theological educator, evangelist and song-writer. He is particularly well known for his hymns, which are very popular among Chinese Christians.

Dear Lord today you call me back, face to face with your love
It makes me feel deeply ashamed
You are even willing to love a person like me
My Lord, your love is truly hard to fathom.

Although I said 'Ah! Lord I love you'
Although I boasted 'I will never leave you'
Before long I deserted you, broke my promises
Saddened you and made you sigh.

But my Lord you were not disheartened
Your wonderful love urged you to seek me out
Until you found me, embraced me in your heart
Made me return to the fold.

Now my Lord I dare not leave your embrace
I dare not fail to live up to your love
I beg you protect me from failure
Until I fully comprehend your love.

Chorus:
My Lord, your love! Wonderful love
Infinitely broad, infinitely deep
It truly is hard for us to fathom
Although I disappointed and saddened you
My Lord, your love sought me back.

32

Rev. David Yang (1900–66), a pastor from northern China, founded the Spiritual Workers' Fellowship, which is a faith mission community. This type of fellowship plays an important role in the expansion of Christianity in the north-western provinces. David Yang later joined the Three Self Patriotic Movement.

So I entrusted myself entirely to him. Praise God.

At that moment the words of Malachi, chapter 4, verse 2, entered my heart: 'But unto you that fear my name shall the Sun of righteousness arise with healing in his wings, and you shall go forth and grow up as calves of the stall'.

In these words of justice I received complete illumination and comfort, and allowed him to come to heal me.

I almost lost consciousness of being in a room, but I knew clearly that I was in the shadow of his wings. Then my whole body was liberated, my perspective on life was transformed and I discovered that tremendous power through my own personal experience.

I no longer felt 'bitterness' and 'sacrifice' but 'eternal comfort'. I had often read these truths in books but only understood them intellectually until now, when I could firmly grasp their true essence in my own bodily experience.

Before, although my mind was filled with joy and praise, I could not express myself, I could just say quietly 'Praise the Lord'.

But now the spirit of joy finally filled my heart I only needed to cry out 'Hallelujah' and my body immediately filled with power, my heart also, my mouth was full of praises, joy surged like the water in oceans and lakes.

I laughed out loud free from all restraints.

33

Rev. Marcus Cheng (1884–1964), pastor, theological educator and army chaplain. Marcus Cheng was a member of the Three Self Patriotic Movement.

The stirring of the Holy Spirit is the effect it produces on human beings. The Holy Spirit co-operates and works with human beings. The wisdom and skills granted by the Holy Spirit are not originally possessed by human beings. Neither were the power and spirit of human beings originally possessed by them.

An official who is moved by the Holy Spirit will be a good official and perform his duties thoroughly. A businessman who is moved by the Holy Spirit will be a good businessman and can promote his business successfully. Workers who are moved by the Holy Spirit work well and are excellent craftsmen. Soldiers who are moved by the Holy Spirit chase out bullies and protect citizens. Preachers moved by the Holy Spirit are excellent preachers, full of power and wisdom.

The Gospel of St John compares the Holy Spirit to water for the following reasons: first, to have the Holy Spirit in the heart is like a cup filled with water; second, if one is filled with the Holy Spirit it is like a cup brimming with water; third, as the Holy Spirit performs great deeds within the human being, it not only brings the individual to perfection but even the whole world. This is like water overflowing from a cup, like a river bursting its banks.

Paul's prayer of blessing says: 'May the touch of the Holy Spirit be with you always, may you have the Holy Spirit in your hearts so you may know your sins. May your hearts be filled with the Holy Spirit, to avoid sins. Above all may the Holy Spirit overflow like a river and accompany you in your work and your great undertakings.'

So whenever we gather together to pray and then before we leave the church I would bless you: may the love and kindness of Jesus Christ always be with you. May the love of God always be with you. May the touch of the Holy Spirit always be with you. Amen.

34

This hymn was written by university students in Beijing in the early 1950s.

> Father, long before the creation of the world
> You chose us in infinite love!
> This sweet, beautiful love, so deep and moving
> Draws us close to Jesus.
> Still it protects us, still it protects us
> From now we are eternally steadfast.
> Still it protects us, still it protects us
> From now we are eternally steadfast.
>
> Although the universe is slowly changing
> Our God is ever constant,
> His loving heart and his words
> Are always steady and firm.
> God's children, God's children,
> We should praise his name.

God's children, God's children
We should praise his name.

The compassion of God is my hymn
My proud boast, my heart's joy;
From beginning to end only pure mercy
Can receive my life, move my heart.
God loves us, God loves us,
He spared not even his Son.
God loves us, God loves us,
He spared not even his Son.

Loving God, together now
We praise your wonderful love,
Until we leave the human world for heaven above
We will always praise you.
Glorify you, glorify you!
Eternally return to God and the Lamb.
Glorify you, glorify you,
Eternally return to God and the Lamb.

35

From a collection of devotional poems by Dr Andrew Song (1902–) author, theologian and poet.

O Lord Jesus
Please abide with me
Dispel my deep loneliness!
No one can be my companion for ever
But you are the Lord who is everywhere
Present at all times
Only you are my dear companion and saviour.

In the long dark night
Along the silent shadowy pathways
I beg you to grasp my hand.
When others have forgotten me
Please remember me in eternity!
In the name of Jesus, Amen.

36

Brother Wong, an old preacher from South China, wrote a devotional booklet including a series of reflections on biblical texts which was sent through one of his colleagues to Hong Kong in 1980. His prayers are full of praise.

'May my meditation be pleasing to him, as I rejoice in the Lord.'
(Psalm 104.34)

> O Lord Jesus, who can love me as you do?
> Through your deeds and labour I have become
> As ripened fruit.
> How blessed it is to share in your glory
> Eternally in your providence.
> I am your treasure
> Product of your arduous labour.

37

Both these extracts arise from the experience of illness. The first is by So Enpei, an acclaimed Christian writer who died of cancer in the early 1980s. The passage was written shortly before her death. The second is by Chen Chunyung (1955–90), a young Methodist preacher in Hong Kong who wrote to his friends after learning that he had terminal cancer in March 1990.

Today I still want to count my blessings in faith; yet today I am also willing to do a little rethinking. There are not only blessings but curses in my life. I deeply feel that I am living under a curse. However it is not a curse given to me personally but one that is given to the whole of humanity as a bondage to all. The whole of humanity groans under this curse of sin. The evil fruit of sin is clearly manifested in every sphere: physical, psychological and other facets of life. Its power extends to every corner. I am but one of the millions who groan together in this furnace of suffering. Yea, the root of suffering cannot be removed in this life and this world. I can only depend on faith in Christ to overcome and transcend suffering.

I trust that God wants me to learn some lessons in my illness. Of course, as I turn around I can comfort others who are living in pain. But more importantly I believe that he wants me to experience him in my illness. At present I desire to learn the lessons of solitude, praise and prayer. Dear brothers and sisters, thank you for sharing the burden of my illness. I sincerely wish that you can share with me this living and true God also.

SECTION FOUR

Nationalism

My purpose in pursuing academic study is to serve the people, not to be served by the people; to do more good things for the people, particularly to serve the great majority of the people who are most vulnerable — the peasants — not to seek personal fame and gain. If my pursuit of learning is mistaken, I pray to God for enlightenment. If it is right, I implore God to help me and give me courage.

Dr Sun Zhonghan (1895–1980), a Christian agronomist who promoted many successful agricultural projects in different parts of China and Taiwan.

One of the major tasks of China in the twentieth century has been to establish itself as an independent, united and self-determining nation. Patriotism and dedication to economic and social progress have been major concerns for many sectors of Chinese society, and these themes are reflected in Christian writings also. It was particularly necessary for Chinese Christians to forge an identity with the Chinese nation since they were often associated with foreigners and accused of being in collusion with imperialism.

38

This statement was made by a group of Christians from two central provinces, Hunan and Hubei, in response to the forceful and sometimes violent Anti-Christian Movement in 1925.

Facing such oppression, what should we do? Should we rely on foreign power? Should we seek the protection of treaties? Should we depend on diplomacy? No, never!

We should never be trapped into these again! To use these things as the foundation for building the church is no better than building a house on sands, where it is bound to collapse in a storm.

What should we do then? Our only option is to rely on our saviour Lord Jesus. We should make a great vow, taking his spirit as ours, his inspiration as ours, his honour or disgrace as our own, his worries and joys as our worries and joys.

In accordance with his teaching we should master our environment, withstand oppression, sacrifice ourselves without complaint and serve others warm-heartedly. We should follow his example in converting others, in our struggle against evil and in our effort to cultivate noble, gracious personalities.

In short, our great goal at present is to establish our church within Christ, so that others will not see the church but will see only Jesus.

39

An open letter to Christians in China, written by the China Christian Council in 1948, at the height of the civil war.

First, we should always defend our freedom to worship and work for God. Many martyrs have sacrificed their lives for this glorious mission. Their blood has become the seeds out of which the churches have grown. We should not allow anyone to take from our hands the happiness gained from the recognition of Christ as our saviour.

Secondly, we should support all efforts to promote political and economic equality. In addition we should seek the realization of this goal through our own conduct. Christ showed great concern and passion for the poor, the distressed, the despised and the oppressed. We should often examine ourselves to see whether we have shown our love for Jesus and our glories to him in our way of life, our relationships with relatives and friends, in the way we fulfil our obligations, our conduct of personal and public business. We should put the teachings into practice; we should not just listen to the teachings and deceive ourselves.

Thirdly, we should pursue the favour of the Lord. The Lord is now giving us his teachings. He urges us to confess our sins, deplore our wrongdoings. He urges us to rely on God's mercy and to pray often. He urges us to preserve the spirit of being united in the Lord, to help each other to display the love of Jesus. If we earnestly seek his guidance he will not leave us disappointed. His abundance of love and grace will leave us lacking nothing. His holy guidance will lead us from victory to victory.

40

By Wong Guoshan, a Little Flock leader in southern China during the late 1940s and early 1950s. He emigrated to the United States, where he became a popular preacher.

In mainland China the spiritual battle is continuing at an even deeper level and needs your support in prayer. This spiritual battle in our own personal life is also continuing, and we should approach the Lord with a respectful and sober mind.

Our Lord is the marshal of the spiritual battle, and the children of God are the troops who follow him. In the past many brothers and sisters fought that wonderful battle and their deeds follow those recorded in the Book of Acts. Now it is time for you to take over the work.

Can you succeed? You should succeed, because all you need to do is to stand beside the Lord, watching him fight on your behalf.

41

Open letter to Christians in China from the Church of Christ in China, 1949.

In this new situation in which it finds itself, the Church should readily accept criticism and engage in its own self-examination.

We must discover our faults and truly repent of them; on no account are we to pride ourselves on our pioneering progressiveness, or with self-satisfaction to blow our own trumpets with regard to such small achievements as we have made in the past.

We must, moreover, develop positive plans: as regards personnel, to train far more leaders of yet higher quality; as regards finance, to hasten on to real implementation of independence and self-support;

As regards social righteousness, courageously to make a determined struggle against the inequities of the economic order and against social evils;

As regards property, to make the fullest use of space available, permitting neither waste nor neglect; and as regards social service and reconstruction, to strive towards making complete the Christian's distinctive contribution.

Apart from these things the Church should stimulate every individual believer, irrespective of the class to which he belongs, to welcome as a citizen, along with his fellow-countrymen throughout the whole country, the advent of these great times, and to assist, each in his own place and to the limit of his strength, in bringing to fulfilment the tasks of reconstruction of this new era.

Our doctors, nurses, teachers and social workers need to develop a yet greater spirit of service and sense of social mission.

Our city and rural pastors and evangelists need better training in social service.

Our Churches must put themselves positively behind the movement for increased production, and raise the people's standard of living; they must take a deeper interest in farmers and labourers, and those in society who are in special need of help; they must demonstrate within the life of their own fellowship the spirit of Christian equality, love and mutual aid; both within and without the Church they must support all kinds of co-operative organizations and movements.

They must seek to bring more abundant life, both spiritual and material to their own members and to all the people they serve.

To sum up, the Christian Church in China must serve the people — individuals, small groups and the masses — with Christian faith, in Christian love.

While it is in the world and while the world lasts, the Church must not for a moment cease its effort, by strenuous struggle, self-denying sacrifice and devout prayer, to bring society as well as individuals nearer to God, for this is the hope which God sets upon mankind.

42

Wang Mingdao (see no. 4).

I say to all believers: in the Bible there is only the truth revealed to us by God, there is not a trace of 'the poison of imperialist thought' . . . we must only believe, spread the Gospel, preach . . . we are ready to pay any price for our faith in God's Word, and will pay any sacrifice to spread his Word . . . we should not retreat or compromise.

The war is truly violent, the battlefield is truly dangerous, but God's glory will be shown here . . . those who glorify him will receive his glory. Hear, the bugles are sounding! See, victory is in sight! Beloved brothers and sisters, let us follow in the Lord's footsteps, hold his great banner high, press forward boldly for his Gospel.

43

This poem was written by Christiana Tsai, who was known as the Queen of the Dark Chamber. She was born into a Manchu noble family and became a Christian in her teens. She contracted an illness which prevented her from having any exposure to light, and she had to live in a darkened room for decades. Yet she remained full of joy and courage. She once wrote: 'Truly in the midst of pain I have found peace, in hardship I have found happiness, in the darkness I have received light. After lying in bed for more than twenty years, I can say that it was worth passing through the shadow of the Valley of Death since I have the joy of knowing Lord Jesus Christ.'

Ah — ancient China!
Four thousand years of culture,
Timeless mountains and rivers:
Your glory has been nurtured in wisdom,
Your sages left a fine reputation to posterity.
Ah — China, we all love you
Ah — beautiful flowing waters
Vast high plateaux and mountain ranges!

We entreat You, Lord God, enable our countrymen to see
That truth and knowledge all come from You.
It is Your voice of revelation
That has sounded from the past.
Mother China — today God is calling you
To help those who will face tribulation,
For they need you.

Heaven bestowed wisdom on our ancient sages
And they saw the true light of heaven from afar;
But they could not see Christ
The yet more beautiful morning star.
Love of the Lord, arising by faith,
Peace of the Lord, awaiting our country
God, heavenly Father, shows us the Way
His truth makes all people free.

I wish every door may be opened,
I wish every walled city may belong
To a New Heaven and a New Earth*
Ruled by Jesus Christ in the highest.
My Lord, my God, let new leaders arise among us,
Make China stand strong and upright,
Make your church
United as one
Victorious over its enemies!

* Revelation 21.1.

SECTION FIVE

Cultural Continuity

Life is like a dream,
Yet the love of God is infinite,
Even if I had a thousand lives,
I would devote them all to serve the Lord.

With clear mind and pure hands,
Good, faithful, loyal,
I am awake,
Waiting to meet the Lord in the air.*

Hymn by Rev. John Su, writer and evangelist living in Hong Kong (see no. 31).

Much Chinese Christian writing is popular in tone and accessible to unsophisticated readers. However some writers make use of more formal literary styles, sometimes adapting classical verse forms, to convey a spirituality with deep roots in Chinese tradition.

---

* 1 Thessalonians 4.17. John Su is referring to the concept of 'rapture' within the context of the dispensationalist view of eschatology.

44

Evening Prayer

This and no. 45 are by Zhang Gongxian, a contemporary Catholic scholar and poet.

Every house is lighted up, darkness falls
We piously kneel to thank the Lord for his kindness.
Looking up to the altar ablaze with colour
We sing a new hymn with beautiful music.
As members of the same church we are of one heart
We sing praises of our Lord with burning passion.
The Lord bestows grace through the Benediction of the Hosts
He grants us peace and good fortune.

The Holy Trinity are the Lords of heaven and earth
They create and save the world, sanctify people.
God creates our physical bodies and gives us souls
The Seven Sacraments are imbued with great mercy.
Everything created by God depends on his protection
Cereals and fruits nourish our bodies.
The Lamb died at Calvary
But the great rite of Mass has lasted till today.

The Heavenly Father is admired by all generations
The Holy Virgin Mother Mary is wondrous.
Now we dedicate ourselves to the Father and the Virgin
Beseech them to renew our souls every day.
All we do must please the Lord
Every action must be careful.
If we do not fail to live up to the Lord's grace
We implore him speedily to remove the traces of sin.

We look to our Holy Mother to give us protection
To pray for us, to open the gate of heaven,
To look down on her children with pity,
To keep us safe from evil spirits.
May the patron saints and guardian angels
Bring us to God's embrace so we may sleep in peace.
Tomorrow we will rise refreshed and work hard,
Return the Lord's love with our love, indebted to his mercy.

45

Morning Prayer

The sun rises shining brightly in the east
The whole world reveals the wonders of the Lord.
A hundred flowers blossom, a hundred birds sing
Everything bears witness to the mystery of God.
Raising our eyes to heaven we see Creation
Hearts full of joy we recite our prayers.
We look to the Lord for illumination and guidance,
In thoughts, words and deeds we follow the path of righteousness.

Every single action starts from ourselves,
It is most important that we fulfil our duties.
We should be gentle and kind in the service of others,
Polite and friendly in our dealings.
We should be honest, sincere, never arrogant,
Help others generously, expect nothing in return.
We should always lead an exemplary life and cultivate merit,
Spread the Holy Teaching like light and salt.

Our Lord toiled in this world
To save people and redeem their sins and crimes.
He had the name 'Son of a carpenter',
He often worked wood with his own hands out of filial duty.
He worked as fisherman, herdsman and healer,
He pitied those in distress and answered their calls.
He set a fine example, rescuing the dying and healing the wounded.
His moral character illuminates and instructs future generations.

I am a Christian and believe the teaching of the Lord,
In every step I follow the Holy Teaching.
We must guard against conceit at any small progress.
Our glories return to the Lord to repay his kindness.
All day we should ponder the Lord's teachings,
Overcome selfishness, laziness and pride.
When we meet difficulties we pray to the Lord
And win glory for the Lord by our good deeds.

46

Rev. Hsi Sin-mor (1835–96) was a classical scholar and an opium addict. He became a Christian and was able to cure himself of his addiction. Later he became a minister closely associated with the China Inland Mission. The references to poverty and oppression in this poem arise from the persecution suffered by many Christians in the nineteenth century.

I am poor because I believe in the Lord,
My heart seems restless;
Yet once I think of the Lord, even though I tramp the roads,
My heart is happy.

I meet oppression because I study the true way,
My heart seems restless;
Yet once I think of the Lord, even though I am bound in chains,
My heart is happy.

I experience trials for the sake of the Gospel,
My heart seems restless;
Yet once I think of the Lord, even though I am beaten with whips,
My heart is happy.

I am tortured for the sake of the Church,
My heart seems restless;
Yet once I think of the Lord, even though I am crucified,
My heart is so happy.

Lord give me peace, Lord give me peace.
The peace granted by the Lord is not that of worldly riches.
People cannot steal it from you, peace is in heaven.

47

From a collection of prayers by Dr F. Y. Zia, a theologian who died recently in Canton, South China.

> I pray that the true God may protect me tonight
> Keep me safe from turmoil and trouble.
> I pray also for my family and friends,
> For all people all over the world —
> I pray the cloud of your compassion
> May cover them and grant them peace.

48

This and the following hymn are by Dr John Sung (see no. 21).

To die completely and live in Christ
Is supreme happiness
Spiritual illumination and joy arise
When passions of the flesh all die away.

The letter of the law and old traditions are all traps
When we are taken to heaven
Satan can no longer condemn us
We have true freedom.

Victory, victory, in the victory of the Lord himself.
Rest in peace, rest in peace, in the peace of the Lord's great power.
Use the authority of the Lord to smash all Satan's plans.
Deepen your insight, pray hard until New Jerusalem is built.

49

Battle of the Spirit

Spiritual fellowship is so sweet
Spiritual joy so mysterious
Prison has become the Garden of Eden
The flames in the furnace break only the chains —
Freedom with the Lord in the air.

The glorious release, freedom of the spirit
No longer suffering in the yoke of the slave.
The great Red Dragon in the sky wants to swallow the boy.
Satan pretends to be an angel of light.

Do not carry your own burden but the yoke of the Lord.
Grasp the Lord's promise and wait till it is fulfilled.
The stirrings of the flesh, evil thoughts of unbelief
Disappear to nothing in the victory of the Lord.

Children of the God of the Final Day
We must pray piously
Stand at the watch-tower, halt any breakthrough.
Whoever is bound on earth is bound in heaven
Whoever is released on earth is released in heaven.

50

A famous hymn by T. C. Chao (see no. 30).

Rise at bright dawn and see the red sun appear in the east
Strong as a warrior, splendid as a bridegroom
In the high sky birds fly
On the wide earth wild flowers are fragrant
Shining on me as I work,
The Holy Father's mercy and light.

I beseech the Holy Father to keep me safe from harm
My behaviour should be kind and good
My expression warm and friendly

I modestly teach the younger generation
Respecting the old, ever obedient,
Expressing the Holy Father's mercy.

I hope today is a good day,
I hope to rely on Jesus every moment,
The clear sky above my head,
No evil thoughts in my mind,
Content with simple clothes,
Happy to eat plain food:
The Lord helps me in every single thing.

51

Song of the Road Home

By Wang Weifan, author, preacher, and teacher of theology at the Nanjing Union Theological Seminary. A collection of Wang's devotional writings entitled Lilies of the Field, *translated into English by P. and J. Wickeri, was published in Hong Kong in 1988.*

The white cloud knows its way back
To the shadow of the hill,
The weary bird knows its path home
To the forest on the hill,
The sun knows where to sink back down
In the distant ocean waters,
I alone am restless
In the distant wilderness.

I have travelled for thousands of miles,
Where does this journey lead?
I have lived for a hundred years,
Where is my final end?
I am weary of wandering;
Although I have an earthly home
My spirit floats in the air,
It is hard to settle down.

Above the distant altar
The birds fly back to their nests,
At the baby swallows' plaintive cry
Their mother knows she should return.
Why do I alone
Find no resting place?
In this infinite universe
It is hard to find a road home.

The lonely shadow of the cross
On a green hill outside the city;
Blazing red poppies dot the fields,
Blood shed in the cause of justice.
The Holy Lamb has already been sacrificed,
The gate of Heaven is opened,
The merciful Father stands at the door
Waiting on the child's return.

The white cloud knows its way
To the shadow of the hill,
The weary bird knows its path
To the forest on the hill,
The sun knows where to sink back down
In the distant ocean waters,
The lost sheep wanders in the wilderness,
Why has it not returned?

The travelling child returns home,
Back to the Father's embrace.
Peacefully resting in You
Could the child bear to leave again?
You, the dwelling place throughout all generations,*
Our eternal home,
Once we abide peacefully in You
We do not wish to leave.

On the green hill — green, green,
The white cloud stops to rest.
In the hill forest — deep, deep,

* Psalm 90.1.

Cultural continuity

The weary bird comes to nest.
The blue waters of the vast ocean
Embrace the red sun.
The father's love, so profound,
Is ever present to the travelling child.

The white cloud knows its way back
To the shadow of the hill,
The weary bird knows its path home
To the forest on the hill,
The sun knows where to sink back down
In the distant ocean waters.
The lost sheep wanders in the wilderness,
Why has it not yet returned?

SECTION SIX

Evangelism

Our brothers from abroad think nothing of travelling thousands of miles to teach the Gospel to the Chinese people. I am Chinese, how can I bear not to spread the Word also? Until my last breath I should preach the Gospel to others.

Liang Fa (1789–1855) was born into a poor family in Guangdong, South China and in 1810 found work with a foreign printing company, where he became interested in Christianity. In 1816 he was baptized, becoming the second Chinese Protestant convert, and from 1819 started to convert others, beginning with his own family. In 1819 he was also ordained and thus became the first Chinese Protestant pastor.

Evangelism by non-Chinese missionaries played an important part in promoting Christianity in China. Later, many Chinese believers themselves developed an ardent evangelistic spirit, mostly directed towards their fellow countrymen. Chinese missionaries also worked in South East Asia and among Chinese communities in the United States and elsewhere. Revivalist meetings proved an effective method of reaching large numbers of people, although personal witness has also been an important element, especially where the Gospel could not be preached openly. The demands of missionary work often led Christians into harsh and dangerous conditions.

52

Bian Yunbo (1925–) wrote a long poem, Dedicated to the Nameless Evangelist, *from which these are extracts. The poem, composed in 1948, inspired many young people to dedicate their lives to preaching the Gospel in remote areas of China. Mr Bian was arrested in the 1950s and imprisoned for many years.*

> It is with my own hands, willingly,
> I cast off the pleasures of the world.
> It is with my own feet, willingly,
> I run forward on the path of suffering!
> So I accept these tears flooding into my heart,
> And when I gaze upon the Crosses at Golgotha, —
> Even though I may die —
> I will never retreat.
>
> You have made many journeys and fought many battles
> You have crossed rivers and mountains,
> Vast plains and wilderness.
> Every day you are coming closer to suffering,
> To many remote and poverty-stricken villages.
> Every day you are further from your comfortable home
> Your sweet dreams, your lovely garden and desk . . .
> Every day you are further away . . . further away . . .
> Yet from this day on you become more determined,
> You strive harder in spite of many difficulties,
> You never give up, not even once.
> Facing storms and heavy rains
> Confronting the tricks and fiery arrows of Satan
> You stand fast at your post, not yielding an inch.

53

An anonymous song written in 1949 in Beijing, just prior to the formation of the People's Republic.

> I beseech you to listen:
> The Chinese people have lived through bitter times

Struggling on the verge of life and death
Flames of war have filled the sky,
Blood flowed through the land,
How can we fail to spread the Gospel?

Hear! The bell of the Gospel is sounding
Arise, arise!
Young people of China let us bear the cross,
Light the torch of revival
Spread the Gospel throughout China
Spread the Gospel throughout the world.

54

By the evangelist John Sung (see no. 21).

People of Fuzhou! Do you know the love of God? In the midst of the nation's suffering God still calls you loudly to repent, to receive his love. You dissolute people, why do you hesitate, why do you not repent?
Dissolute people! Repent soon!
Surely you do not love the world so much that you are ready to die, still not enlightened, still unrepentant?
Dissolute people, repent soon!

55

Part of a letter written by a Chinese pastor in America who visited China in 1988 after an absence of forty years. To his delight he succeeded in meeting a few of his former colleagues from Shanghai. Many had died, but some survivors were still active, working to spread the Gospel in the remote province of Xinjiang.

More than thirty years ago these spiritual soldiers of Christ were about to set out for the distant border regions of Xinjiang. I saw them off from Shanghai and helped them in every respect.

Some brothers and sisters wanted to make offerings to them, so I helped to transfer the funds.

When the time of persecution came, they all died in prison, one by one. At this time I went to their graves and put a little earth on the mounds.

So many brothers and sisters poured out their blood on this earth of the border regions. There will come a day when God will reward them many times over, remembering their suffering and their destruction.

56

A poem of the North-West Spiritual Fellowship

This poem and no. 57 were written by members of the North-West Spiritual Workers' Fellowship, a missionary organization which works to establish the Gospel among the non-Han peoples in the north-west of China. The group was formed in the late 1940s and banned in the early 1950s. However, their work has continued despite the unfavourable political climate of the last decades. Many house churches in Xinjiang owe their existence to the efforts of this group.

When we look westwards we see a vast barren country
The Lord is always so concerned and asks:
'Who is willing to go there for me?'

We shed tears in our enthusiasm
The blood burns in our veins
We will hold high the banner of Christ to save the lost sheep.

57

Ambassadors of the Heavenly Kingdom

Ambassadors of the Heavenly Kingdom are called
To save lost souls
And face the sufferings of a long journey.

We wear wind and dust as our clothes
We walk without staves
We have no gold or silver in our purses
We learn from the birds in the sky
We rely on God for all our needs.

We appear to be poor but we make others rich.
We appear to have nothing,
But we have more than others in every respect.
We commend the new life of Christ
We advocate the true Gospel of the Cross.
Wherever we go we leave beautiful footprints,
Wherever we go we open the door of grace.

We should lead sinners back to the Lord,
Lead the Prodigal Son to see God the Father.
We do our work with the strength of the Spirit,
Not with our tongues, teeth and lips.
We are ready to sacrifice our lives for the love of others,
Not relying on paper, pens and essays.
We will follow the instructions of the Lord to call the common people,
We will respect the Lord's wish to save people from damnation.
Not until the flags of love are planted all over the world
Should we think that we have done our duty.

58

These two poems were written towards the end of the Second World War by Rev. Wang Yunshu, who was one of the first Chinese missionaries to work overseas. He tried to establish churches among Chinese and Filipinos, but suffered much from illness and isolation.

Evangelism

Appealing to God

Left alone in this tragic island I feel wretched
My body freezes, it seems impossible I can ever return home
Continuous wars have interrupted all communications
Frequent slanders have made my illness even worse.

Tossing and turning in my sick-bed I often dream of home
Only in my long exile do I appreciate the affection of marriage
Since I know that I cannot escape these miseries by myself
I rise sadly in the night, appealing to you my God, Father.

In the Wild Philippines

It is eight years since I came to the south, bearing the Cross
Now I have drunk the cup of bitterness my faith is even stronger
In dangerous times, a chaotic world and endless wars
Without friends, without relatives, I am seriously ill.

Even if my home exists I cannot return
It is sweet to follow you even if I must leave the world
I will be happy to depart when I have completed my duties
Let my bones be buried in the wild Philippines.

59

Journey Home with the Cross

By Simon Zhao (see no. 1).

The yearning love of my heart
Longs to walk the road of the Cross
The era of fire urges me to walk
I cannot hesitate for a moment,
I firmly believe the bloody road of the Cross
Is the only aim of my life.

This homeward journey with the Cross
Is full of pain and sudden changes
There are times of weakness and desolation
There are many tears and sorrows
But the Lord always stretches his kind hand
To lead me on the way forward.

I would rather choose the suffering of the Cross
Than a peaceful easy road.
I would rather shed my blood on the road to Xinjiang
Than drag out an ignoble existence in my home town.
I would rather suffer the humiliation of the Cross
To share the bitter cup with the Lord.

The journey home with the Cross is a long and perilous march
There are blood, tears and battles
Many storms and many perils.
For many years the blood of the martyrs
Has been shed on this same journey.

SECTION SEVEN

Longer articles

The church shall teach her members to agree to differ, but resolve to love.

Rev. Dr Timothy Liu Ting-Fan (1892–1947). This was his closing remark at the First Chinese Christian Conference, held in Shanghai in 1922.

In China, as in other countries, Christians harbour differences of opinion on doctrinal, political and other issues. This section presents longer extracts from Bishop K. H. Ting, the most eminent figure in the official Chinese Church, and Watchman Nee, who refused all co-operation with it. Also included are two descriptions of Christianity at grass-roots level and some reactions to the massacre of 4 June 1989. Chinese Christianity is not a monolithic entity but a spectrum rich in spirituality.

60

'Give ye them to eat'

(Luke 9.12-17)

Bishop K. H. Ting (1915–) is the leading figure of the official Chinese Protestant Church. He has held numerous senior positions in the Three Self Movement, the China Christian Council, in the Nanjing Theological Seminary and in national political bodies. He has also represented the Chinese Church on many delegations outside China. His speeches and articles have been widely printed and also translated into English. This passage is adapted from a sermon delivered by Bishop Ting at the Timothy Eaton Memorial Church, Toronto, Canada on 4 November 1979.

We have just read the wonderful story in Luke of the feeding of the five thousand. There are a few things to which I wish to call your attention.

First, the disciples thought that Christ's work consisted only of talking about the Kingdom. As to the question of feeding the multitude, it was none of his business and, therefore, none of their business either. They said to send the crowd away, let them go their own ways and get whatever food they could. But Christ said, 'Give ye them to eat'. The disciples were actually advocating the principle of each looking after themselves; that is, each doing his or her own thing. If this is put into practice, as indeed it has been in China and elsewhere, the result is inevitably that the strong and mighty dominate and the common people become their victims. This ends up in a full-fledged capitalism which is defined by a world renowned economist as 'the extraordinary belief that for the nastiest of the motives the nastiest of men will somehow work for the benefit of us all'. We know that this has not worked out that way.

Second, in order to feed the people, Christ instructed the disciples that the multitude be divided into groups of roughly fifty people each and that they sit in groups rather than walk about in disorder. Since it was Christ that said that, I suppose people would be kind enough not to call that regimentation or curtailment of individual freedom. Let us say it is some necessary discouragement of individualism, a certain amount of programme, planning and organization. And we know from our experience in China that this is necessary.

Third, let us note that Christ looked up to heaven, blessed the food, broke the bread and gave the food to the disciples to set before the multitude. My guess is that there were many views and opinions in the multitude, as regards the person of Jesus Christ. But Christ respected them all. His care was for the whole multitude, indeed all of humanity, not just those in the crowd who knew him personally. God is so great that it would not be true to his nature for his love and care to be reserved only for those who consciously profess his name. He does not mind terribly that there are those who for some reason cannot acknowledge, but must deny, his name.

Fourth, although it was far from being a banquet, there was no shortage. Nobody needed to suffer from starvation. What a relief it must be for parents to know their children would not need to go to bed that night in hunger. And that is an important part of the meaning of the word liberation. When I say China is a liberated country, I do have in mind the fact that, through planning and organization, we are able to feed almost one-fourth of the humanity with the food produced on only one-seventh of the arable land of the earth. It is not a miracle like Christ's but it is an achievement we want to thank God for.

Fifth, let us note that there were twelve left-over basketfuls of food but nothing was said of what happened to them. Where did they go? Were they thrown away? Or just left there to be devoured by animals which came by night? Or sold to someone who could pay a good price and who hoarded it up until there was a shortage of grain and the market price went up, and then sold out, so that the rich became richer and the poor became poorer? The biblical silence on the disposal of the left-over food comes to us by what the Bible says, but sometimes it also comes to us by what the Bible refrains from saying. Here is a guiding principle for our bible study: there is sometimes a still small voice in biblical silence. Is it possible that the silence of St Luke's Gospel on this very point means that the Holy Spirit is leading us into seeing that the problem was not really solved by feeding five thousand people? What can twelve basketfuls of food do to relieve 50 thousand, the

500 thousand and the 5 or even 50 million poor people of their hunger? So this biblical silence has become for us a symbol of unfinished responsibility, of the unhelpfulness of mere philanthropy in a world which is producing poverty and hunger much faster than our kind-hearted philanthropist can catch up with. Traditional ethics only look at the actors, the hungry men and women on the streets, the beggars, the thieves and the robbers; but the mystery of the twelve basketfuls urges us to examine the social order.

Our good earth can produce enough for everybody's needs but cannot produce enough for everybody's greed. How are we to distribute wealth and opportunities more justly? That is the question the gospel story has raised for us.

When I was a primary school student I lived in Shanghai, and I know something of how the wealthy lived in those days. Several miles away was Yangzhou, an area so poor that whenever there was a drought — and that was quite often — men and women from Yangzhou would come to Shanghai, bare-footed and in rags to seek work. They were so bony and lifeless that their very appearance was frightening to me. They did not really expect any wages, just enough food to survive. And many could find neither work nor food. They became beggars. Some of them died on the streets because of hunger and cold. Girls were sold into prostitution. For boys, to be accepted as an apprentice in a barber shop was considered the best of luck. These were the down-trodden, and they constituted the majority.

Two years ago I visited Yangzhou again. There are no longer any landlords to extort exorbitant rentals from the peasants. There is hydraulic irrigation now. People are living in brick houses rather than huts of mud. Men and women are studying, from kindergarten to university, or are working in factories or on the farm. Many women factory workers wear leather shoes and watches. Some of them wear woollen trousers and Dacron shirts, and ride their own bikes to work. These things may not mean anything to Westerners, but to them it is a tremendous change. When I heard their laughter, I was almost in tears, because I was thinking of the plight of their forebears. How I wished to tell young people there about what I had seen as a boy so that they would not forget the past.

I think Christians have good reason to be concerned with the question of material distribution. After Christ's resurrection, he walked to Emmaus with two of his disciples. Remember that it was not when he was expounding the scriptures to them, warming their hearts, that they came to know who he was. Nor was it when he sat down to eat with them. Only when he took the bread and blessed it and gave the bread to them did their eyes open and come to know him as the Christ. Could we not then say that the distribution of the bread to humanity really contains something of the sacrament? The way wealth and opportunities are distributed in society does have a lot to do with the manifestation of Jesus Christ to men and women.

We know that the God Jesus Christ came to reveal to us is a God who is at the same time living and almighty. If people take their conception of God seriously, this sort of God is not very easy to visualize. For people who have experienced injustice and deprivation and suffering, it is much easier to visualize a God who is loving but not almighty, or a God who is almighty but not loving, or a God who is neither loving nor almighty. And yet we insist that God is both loving and almighty in spite of the evils and sufferings around us. Because it is so demanding, people find it hard to hold to this Christian conception of God. They are more attracted to the death-of-God hypothesis. The death of God as a theological fad lasted briefly but the death of God as a working philosophy of life is spreading. A Jewish rabbi commented: 'When I say we live in the time of the death of God, I mean that the thread uniting God and humanity, heaven and earth has been broken. We stand in a cold, silent, unfeeling cosmos, unaided by any purposeful power beyond our own resources. After Auschwitz, what else can a Jew say about God?'

Here in a naked way we see how social, economic, and political injustice eats away at man's faith in a God who is at once almighty and loving. It is only the achievement of a healthier social system and a fairer distribution of the world's goods, with all the prosperity, peace, joy and progress it entails, that will enable men and women to find some reasonableness in our Christian conception of God, of the God who is the Father Almighty, and to find causes for giving thanks to that God. It is easy to imagine how difficult it is for people undergoing perpetual suffering to sense much of what the New Testament says. Some Christians in China, in looking back on the miserable life they led in the old days, like to recall how difficult it was to make sense out of the words 'put away anxious thoughts about food and drinks to keep you alive and clothes to cover your body'. The question that haunted them was not so much life after death as life after birth. It is only today that they can free themselves of these tormenting anxieties and begin to learn to feel at home in this, our Father's world.

Thus the question of distribution has an important evangelistic dimension which we must not overlook. The water which runs through the hydraulic irrigation system in Yangzhou is cold of course, but I like to think of the warmth it brings to human life. Thus we see that material things are not necessarily evil, and that they can be a channel for transmitting in some way a grace of God. This is a Sacrament in the rudimentary sense of the word, for these material things now represent and convey something of God's love and care to people.

We are serious when we say this is God's world. We mean that this world is not Satan's. The thread uniting God and humanity, heaven and earth, has not been broken, and we do not stand in a cold, silent, unfeeling cosmos. It means God the Father Almighty, the all-loving and all-powerful God, God the Creator, is today carrying on his work of Creation to its completion. What human beings do with our hands and minds is meaningful, and should not be destroyed at the end of history, but be received by Christ, be transfigured, perfected and made acceptable to God. Thomas Aquinas said that Grace does not supplant, but perfects, nature. For the Incarnation of the Son of God to have happened at all means that there is not a total disparity between God and the world, between grace and nature. To say that man is fallen is to say that he is not in his proper state; the state where he belongs, the state for which he is made. It certainly does not mean that all his work is for nothing. The Incarnation of the Son of God has surely made more of an impact on humanity than the Fall of Adam. Human solidarity with Christ is more universal and more powerful than human solidarity with Adam through sin. We believe in a universality of divine grace. We look at the world in the splendour of the Ascended Christ. What human beings do to promote community, to make love more available to the masses of our people, is in consonance with God's work of Creation, Redemption and Sanctification. God himself — the Father, the Son, and the Holy Spirit — reveals the image of the loving community after which humanity was created, and is moving in the direction of recovering that image. The creation itself will be set free from bondage and obtain the glorious liberty of the children of God.

This is how we look at human aspirations, movements and struggles. This is the source of our optimism and thanksgiving.

The German poet Bertolt Brecht said the following about a humanly unlivable society:

> Those who take the meat from the able
> Teach contentment.
> Those for whom the taxes are destined
> Demand sacrifice.
> Those who eat their fill speak to the hungry
> Of the wonderful time to come.
> Those who lead the country into the abyss
> Call ruling too difficult
> For ordinary folk.

The feeding of the five thousand takes us to an entirely different world — the world which is a community of sharing, where life is so organized that men and women can be brothers and sisters to each other. As we live our daily life, may the vision of this coming world sustain us in the fellowship of faith, hope and love.

61

The Goal of the Gospel

Watchman Nee (see no. 22)

For our final chapter we will take as our starting-point an incident in the Gospels that occurs under the very shadow of the Cross — an incident that, in its details, is at once historic and prophetic. 'While he was in Bethany in the house of Simon the leper, as he sat at meat, there came a woman having an alabaster cruse of ointment of spikenard very costly; and she brake the cruse, and poured it over his head . . . Jesus said . . . Verily I say unto you, Wheresoever the gospel shall be preached throughout the whole world, that also which this woman hath done shall be spoken of for a memorial of her' (Mark 14.3, 6, 9).

Thus the Lord ordained that the story of Mary anointing Him

with that costly ointment should always accompany the story of the Gospel; that what Mary has done should always be coupled with what the Lord has done. That is His own statement. What does He intend that we should understand of it?

I think we all know the story of Mary's action well. From the details given in John chapter 12, where the incident follows not long after her brother's restoration to life, we may gather that the family was not a specially wealthy one. The sisters had to work in the house themselves, for we are told that at this feast 'Martha also served' (John 12.2 and compare Luke 10.40).

The author here takes the fairly common view that the 'house of Simon the leper' was the home of Mary, Martha and Lazarus, Simon presumably also being a relative of the two sisters.

No doubt every penny mattered to them. Yet one of those sisters, Mary, having among her treasure an alabaster cruse containing three hundred pence worth of ointment, expended the whole thing on the Lord. Human reasoning said this was really too much: it was giving the Lord more than His due. That is why Judas took the lead, and the other disciples supported him, in voicing a general complaint that Mary's action was a wasteful one.

Waste

'But there were some that had indignation among themselves saying, To what purpose hath this waste of the ointment been made? For this ointment might have been sold for above three hundred pence and given to the poor. And they murmured against her' (Mark 14.4, 5). These words bring us to what I believe the Lord would have us consider finally together, namely, that which is signified by the little word 'waste'.

What is waste? Waste means, among other things, giving more than is necessary. If a shilling will do and you give a pound, it is a waste. If two grams will do and you give a kilogram, it is a waste. If three days will suffice to finish a task well enough and you lavish five days or a week on it, it is a waste. Waste means that you give something too much for something too little. If someone is receiving more than he is considered to be worth, then that is waste.

But remember, we are dealing here with something which the Lord said was to go out with the Gospel, wherever that Gospel should be carried. Why? Because He intends that the preaching of the Gospel should issue something along the very lines of the action of Mary here, namely, that people should come to Him and waste themselves on Him. This is the result that He is seeking.

We must look at this question of wasting on the Lord from two angles: that of Judas (John 12.4–6) and that of the other disciples (Matthew 26.8, 9); and for our present purpose we will run together the parallel accounts.

All the twelve thought it a waste. To Judas of course, who had never called Jesus 'Lord', everything that was poured out upon Him was waste. Not only was ointment waste; even water would have been waste. Here Judas stands for the world. In the world's estimation the service of the Lord, and our giving ourselves to Him for such service, is sheer waste. He has never been loved, never had a place in the hearts of the world, so any giving to Him is a waste. Many say: 'Such-and-such a man could make good in the world if only he were not a Christian!' Because a man has some natural talent or other asset in the world's eyes, they count it a shame for him to be serving the Lord. They think such people are really too good for the Lord. 'What waste of a useful life!' they say.

Let me give a personal instance. In 1929 I returned from Shanghai to my home town of Foochow. One day I was walking along the street with a stick, very weak and in broken health, and I met one of my old college professors. He took me into a teashop where we sat down. He looked at me from head to foot and from foot to head, and then he said: 'Now look here; during your college days we thought a good deal of you, and we had hopes that you would achieve something great. *Do you mean to tell me that this is what you are?*' Looking at me with penetrating eyes, he asked that very pointed question. I must confess that, on hearing it, my first desire was to break down and weep. My career, my health, everything had gone, and here was my old professor who taught me law in the school, asking me: 'Are you still in this condition, with no success, no progress, nothing to show?'

But the very next moment — and I have to admit that in all my life it was the first time — I really knew what it meant to have the 'Spirit of glory' resting upon me. The thought of being able to pour out my life for my Lord flooded my soul with glory. Nothing short of the Spirit of glory was on me then. I could look up and without a reservation say, 'Lord, I praise Thee! This is the best thing possible; it is the right course that I have chosen!' To my professor it seemed a total waste to serve the Lord; but that is what the Gospel is for — to bring each one of us to a true estimate of His worth.

Judas felt it a waste. 'We could manage better with the money by using it in some other way. There are plenty of poor people. Why not rather give it for charity, do some social service for their uplift, help the poor in some practical way? Why pour it out at the feet of Jesus?' (see John 12.4–6). That is always the way the world reasons. 'Can you not find a better employment with yourself than this? It is going a bit too far to give yourself altogether to the Lord!'

But if the Lord is worthy, then how can it be a waste? He is worthy to be so served. He is worthy for me to be His prisoner. He is worthy for me just to live for Him. *He is worthy!* What the world says about this does not matter. The Lord says: 'Do not trouble her'. So let us not be troubled. Men may say what they like, but we can stand on this ground, that the Lord said, 'It is a good work. Every true work is not done on the poor; every true work is done to Me.' When once our eyes have been opened to the real worth of our Lord Jesus, *nothing* is too good for Him.

But I do not want to dwell too much on Judas. Let us go on to see what was the attitude of the other disciples, because their reaction affects us even more than does his. We do not greatly mind what the world is saying; we can stand that, but we do very much mind what other Christians are saying who ought to understand. And yet we find that they said the same thing as Judas; and they not only said it but they were very upset, very indignant about it. 'When the disciples saw it, they had indignation, saying, To what purpose is this waste? For this ointment might have been sold for much, and given to the poor' (Matthew 26.8, 9).

Of course we know that the attitude of mind is all too common among Christians which says, 'Get all you can for as little as possible'. That however is not what is in view here, but something deeper. Let me illustrate. Has someone been telling you that you are wasting your life by sitting still and not doing much? They say, 'Here are people who ought to get out into this or that kind of work. They could be used to help this or that group of people. Why are they not more active?' — and in saying so, their whole idea is *use*. Everything ought to be used to the full in ways they understand.

The goal of the Gospel

There are those who have been very concerned with some dear servants of the Lord on this very ground, that they are apparently not *doing* enough. They could do so much more, they think, if they could secure an entry somewhere and enjoy a greater acceptance and prominence in certain circles. They could then be used in a far greater way. I have spoken already of a sister whom I knew for a long time and who, I think, is the one by whom I have been helped most. She was used of the Lord in a very real way during those years when I was associated with her, though to some of us at the time this was not so apparent. The one concern in my heart was this: 'She is not used!' Constantly I said to myself, 'Why does she not get out and take some meetings, go somewhere, do something? It is a waste for her to be living in that small village with nothing happening!' Sometimes, when I went to see her, I almost shouted at her. I said, 'No one knows the Lord as you do. You know the Book in a most living way. Do you not see the need around? Why don't you *do* something? It is a waste of time, a waste of energy, a waste of money, a waste of everything, just sitting here and doing nothing!'

But no, brethren, that is not the first thing with the Lord. He wants you and me to be used, certainly. God forbid that I should preach inactivity, or seek to justify a complacent attitude to the world's need. As Jesus Himself says here, 'the gospel shall be preached throughout the whole world'. But the question is one of emphasis. Looking back today, I realize how greatly the Lord was in fact using that dear sister to speak to a number of us who, as young men, were at that time in His training school for this very work of the Gospel. I cannot thank God enough for her and for the influence of her life upon me.

What, then, is the secret? Clearly it is this, that in approving Mary's action at Bethany, the Lord Jesus was laying down one thing as a basis of all service; that you pour out all you have, your very self, *unto Him*; and if that should be all He allows you to do, that is enough. It is not first of all a question of whether 'the poor' have been helped or not. That will follow, but the first question is: Has the Lord been satisfied?

There is many a meeting we might address, many a convention at which we might minister, many a Gospel campaign in which we might have a share. It is not that we are unable to do it. We could labour and be used to the full; but the Lord is not so concerned about our ceaseless occupation in work for Him. That is not His first object. The service of the Lord is not to be measured by tangible results. No, my friends, the Lord's first concern is with our position at His feet and our anointing of His head. Whatever we have as an 'alabaster box': the most precious thing, the thing dearest in the world to us — yes, let me say it, *the outflow from us of a life that is produced by the very Cross itself* — we give that all up *to the Lord*. To some, even of those who should understand, it seems a waste; but that is what He seeks above all. Often enough the giving to Him will be in tireless service, but He reserves to Himself the right to suspend the service for a time, in order to discover to us whether it is that, or Himself, that holds us.

Ministering to His pleasure

'Wheresoever the gospel shall be preached . . . that also which this woman hath done shall be spoken of' (Mark 14.9).

Why did the Lord say this? Because the Gospel is meant to produce this. It is what the Gospel is for. The Gospel is not just to satisfy sinners. Praise the Lord, sinners will be satisfied! But their satisfaction is, we may say, a blessed by-product of the Gospel and not its primary aim. The Gospel is preached in the first place so that *the Lord* may be satisfied.

I am afraid we lay too much emphasis on the good of sinners and we have not sufficiently appreciated what the Lord has in view as His goal. We have been thinking how the sinner will fare if there is no Gospel, but that is not the main consideration. Yes, Praise God! the sinner has his part. God meets his need and showers him with blessings; but that is not the most important thing. The first thing is this, that everything should be to the satisfaction of the Son of God. It is only when He is satisfied that we shall be satisfied and the sinner will be satisfied. I have never met a soul who has set out to satisfy the Lord and has not been satisfied himself. It is impossible. Our satisfaction comes unfailingly when we satisfy Him first.

But we have to remember this, that He will never be satisfied without our 'wasting' ourselves upon Him. Have you ever given too much to the Lord? May I tell you something? One lesson some of us have come to learn is this, that in divine service the principle of waste is the principle of power. The principle which determines usefulness is the very principle of scattering. Real usefulness in the hand of God is measured in terms of 'waste'. The more you think you can *do*, and the more you empty your gifts up to the very limit (and some even go over the limit!) in order to do it, the more you find that you are applying the principle of the world and not of the Lord. God's ways with us are all designed to establish in us this other principle, namely, that our work *for* Him springs out of our ministering *to* Him. I do not mean that we are going to do nothing; but the first thing for us must be the Lord Himself, not His work.

But we must come down to very practical issues. You say: 'I have given up a position; I have given up a ministry; I have forgone certain attractive possibilities of a bright future, in order to go on with the Lord in this way. Now I try to serve Him. Sometimes it seems that the Lord hears me, and sometimes He keeps me waiting for a definite answer. Sometimes He uses me, but sometimes it seems that He passes me by. Then, when this is so, I compare myself with that other fellow who is in a certain big system. He too had a bright future, but he has never given it up. He continues on and he serves the Lord. He sees souls saved and the Lord blesses his ministry. He is successful — I do not mean materially, but spiritually — and I sometimes think he looks more like a Christian than I do, so happy, so satisfied. After all, what do I get out of this? He has a good time; I have all the bad time. He has never gone this way, and yet he has much that Christians today regard as spiritual prosperity, while I have all sorts of complications coming to me. What is the meaning of it all? Am I wasting my life? Have I really given too much?

So there is your problem. You feel that were you to follow in that other brother's steps — were you, shall we say, to consecrate yourself enough for the blessing but not enough for the trouble, enough for the Lord to use you but not enough for Him to shut you up — all would be perfectly all right. But would it? You know quite well that it would not.

Take your eyes off that other man! Look at your Lord, and ask yourself again what it is that *He* values most highly. The principle of waste is the principle that He would have govern us. 'She is doing this *for Me.*' True satisfaction is brought to the heart of God when we are really, as people would think, 'wasting' ourselves upon Him. It seems as though we are giving too much and getting nothing — and *that* is the secret of pleasing God.

Oh, friends, what are we seeking? Do we seek for 'use' as those disciples did? They wanted to make every penny of those three hundred pence go to its full length. The whole question was one of obvious 'usefulness' to God in terms that could be measured and put on record. The Lord waits to hear us say: 'Lord, I do not mind about that. If I can only please *Thee*, it is enough.'

Anointing Him beforehand

'Let her alone; why trouble ye her? she hath wrought a good work on me. For ye have the poor always with you, and whensoever ye will ye can do them good: but me ye have not always. She hath done what she could: she hath anointed my body aforehand for the burying' (Mark 14.6–8).

In these verses the Lord Jesus introduces a time-factor with the word 'beforehand', and this is something of which we can have a new application today, for it is as important to us now as it was to her then. We all know that in the age to come we shall be called to a greater work — not to inactivity. 'Well done, good and faithful servant: thou hast been faithful over a few things, I will set thee over many things: enter thou into the joy of thy lord' (Matthew 25.21; and compare Matthew 24.47 and Luke 19.17). Yes, there will be a greater work; for the work of God's house will go on, just as in the story the care of the poor went on. The poor would always be with them, but they could not always have Him. There was something, represented by this pouring out of the ointment, which Mary had to do *beforehand* or she would have no later opportunity. I believe that in that day we shall all love Him as we have never done now, but yet that will be most blessed for those who have poured out their all upon the Lord today. When we see Him face to face, I trust that we shall all break and pour out everything for Him. But *today* — what are we doing *today*?

Several days after Mary broke the alabaster box and poured the ointment on Jesus' head, there were some women who went early in the morning to anoint the body of the Lord. Did they do it? Did they succeed in their purpose on that first day of the week? No, there was only one soul who succeeded in anointing the Lord, and it was Mary, who anointed Him beforehand. The others never did it, for He had risen. Now I suggest that, in just such a way, the matter of time may be supremely important to us also, and that for us the question above all questions is: *What am I doing to the Lord today?*

Have our eyes been opened to see the preciousness of the One whom we are serving? Have we come to see that nothing less than the dearest, the costliest, the most precious, is fit for Him? Have we recognized that working for the poor, working for the benefit of the world, working for the souls of men and for the eternal good of the sinner — all these so necessary and valuable things — are right only if they are in their place? In themselves, as things apart, they are as nothing compared with work that is done *to the Lord*.

The Lord has to open our eyes to His worth. If there is in the world some precious art treasure, and I pay the high price asked for it, be it one thousand, ten thousand, or even 50 thousand pounds, dare anyone say it is a waste? The idea of waste only comes into our Christianity when we underestimate the worth of our Lord. The whole question is: How precious is He to us now? If we do not think much of Him, then of course to give Him anything at all, however small, will seem to us a wicked waste. But when He is really precious to our souls, nothing will be too good, nothing too costly for Him; everything we have, our dearest, our most priceless treasure, we shall pour out upon Him, and we shall not count it a shame to have done so.

Of Mary the Lord said: 'She hath done what she could'. What does that mean? It means that she had given up her all. She had kept nothing in reserve for a future day. She had lavished on Him all she had; and yet on the resurrection morning she had no reason to regret her extravagance. And the Lord will not be satisfied with anything less from us than that we too should have done 'what we could'. By this, remember, I do not mean the expenditure of our effort and energy in trying to do something for Him, for that is not the point here. What the Lord Jesus looks for in us is a life laid at His feet, and that in view of His death and burial and of a future day. His burial was already in view that day in the home in Bethany. Today it is His crowning that is in view, when He shall be acclaimed in glory as the Anointed One, the Christ of God. Yes, then we shall pour out our all upon Him! But it is a precious thing — indeed it is a far more precious thing to Him — that we should anoint Him now, not with any material oil but with something costly, something from our hearts.

That which is merely external and superficial has no place here. It has already been dealt with by the Cross, and we have given our consent to God's judgement upon it and learnt to know in experience its cutting off. What God is demanding of us now is represented by that flask of alabaster: something mined from the depths, something turned and chased and wrought upon, something that, because it is so truly of the Lord, we cherish as Mary cherished that flask, and we would not, we dare not break it. It comes now from the heart, from the depth of our being; and we come to the Lord with that, and we break it and pour it out and say: 'Lord, here it is. It is all Yours, because You are worthy!' — and the Lord has got what He desired. May He receive such an annointing from us *today*.

Fragrance

'And the house was filled with the odour of the ointment' (John 12.3). By the breaking of that flask and the anointing of the Lord Jesus, the house was pervaded with the sweetest fragrance. Everyone could smell it and none could be unaware of it. What is the significance of this?

Whenever you meet someone who has really suffered — someone who has gone through experiences with the Lord that have brought limitation, and who, instead of trying to break free in order to be 'used', has been willing to be imprisoned by Him and has thus learned to find satisfaction in the Lord and nowhere else — then immediately you become aware of something. Immediately your spiritual senses detect a sweet savour of Christ. Something has been crushed, something has been broken in that life, and so you smell the odour. The odour that filled the house that day in Bethany still fills the Church today; Mary's fragrance never passes. It needed but one stroke to break the flask for the Lord, but her action — that unreserved giving and the fragrance of that anointing — abides.

We are speaking here of what we are; not of what we do or what we preach. Perhaps you may have been asking the Lord for a long time that He will be pleased to use you in such a way as to impart impressions of Himself to others. That prayer is not exactly for the gift of preaching or teaching. It is rather that you might be able, in your touch with others, to impart God, the presence of God, the sense of God. Let me tell you, dear friends, you cannot produce such impressions of God upon others without the breaking of everything, even your most precious possessions, at the feet of the Lord Jesus.

But if once that point is reached, you may or may not seem to be much used in an outward way, but God will begin to use you to create a hunger in others. People will scent Christ in you. The most unlikely people will detect that. They will sense that here is one who has gone with the Lord, one who has suffered, one who has not moved freely, independently, but who has known what it is to subject everything to Him. That kind of life creates impressions, and impressions create hunger, and hunger provokes men to go on seeking until they are brought by divine revelation into fullness of life in Christ.

God does not set us here first of all to preach or to do work for Him. The first thing for which He sets us here is to create in others a hunger for Himself. That is, after all, what prepares the soil for the preaching.

If you set a delicious cake in front of two men who have just had a heavy meal, what will be their reaction? They will talk about it, admire its appearance, discuss the recipe, argue about the cost — do everything in fact but eat it! But if they are truly hungry it will not be very long before that cake is gone. And so it is with the things of the Spirit. No true work will ever begin in a life without first of all a sense of need being created. But how can this be done? We cannot inject spiritual appetite by force into others; we cannot compel people to be hungry. Hunger has to be created, and it can be created in others only by those who carry with them the impression of God.

I always like to think of the words of that 'great woman' of Shunem. Speaking of the prophet, whom she had observed but whom she did not know well, she said; 'Behold now, I perceive that this is an holy man of God, which passeth by us continually' (2 Kings 4.9). It was not what Elisha said or did that conveyed that impression, but what he was. By his merely passing by she could detect something; she could *see*. What are people sensing about us? We may leave many kinds of impressions: we may leave the impression that we are clever, that we are gifted, that *we* are this or that or the other. But no, the impression left by Elisha was an impression of God Himself.

This matter of our impact upon others turns upon one thing, and that is the working of the Cross in us with regard to the pleasure of the heart of God. It demands that I seek His pleasure, that

I seek to satisfy Him only, and I do not mind how much it costs me to do so. The sister of whom I have spoken came once into a situation that was very difficult for her; I mean, it was costing her everything. I was with her at the time, and together we knelt down and prayed with wet eyes. Looking up she said: 'Lord, I am willing to break my heart in order that I may satisfy Thy heart!' To talk thus of heartbreak might with many of us be merely romantic sentiment, but in the particular situation in which she was, it meant to her just that.

There must be something — a willingness to yield, a breaking and a pouring out of everything to Him — which gives release to that fragrance of Christ and produces in other lives an awareness of need, drawing them out and on to know the Lord. This is what I feel to be the heart of everything. The Gospel has as its one object the producing in us sinners of a condition that will satisfy the heart of our God. In order that He may have that, we come to Him with all we have, all we are — yes, even the most cherished things in our spiritual experience — and we make known to Him: 'Lord, I am willing to let go all of this for You: not just for Your work, not for Your children, not for anything else at all, but altogether and only for Yourself!'

Oh, to be wasted! It is a blessed thing to be wasted for the Lord. So many who have been prominent in the Christian world know nothing of this. Many of us have been used to the full — have been used, I would say, too much — but we do not know what it means to be 'wasted on God'. We like to be always 'on the go': the Lord would sometimes prefer to have us in prison. We think in terms of apostolic journeys: God dares to put His greatest ambassador in chains.

'But thanks be unto God, which always leadeth us in triumph in Christ, and maketh manifest through us the savour of his knowledge in every place' (2 Corinthians 2.14).

'And the house was filled with the odour of the ointment' (John 12.3).

The Lord grant us grace that we may learn how to please Him. When, like Paul, we make this our supreme aim (2 Corinthians 5.9), the Gospel will have achieved its end.

62

A Christian Village

Raymond Fung

This and no. 63 are descriptions of grass-roots Christianity in China written in the early 1980s by Raymond Fung and published by the World Council of Churches.

I am eighteen years old. My parents, foster parents actually, have asked me to tell you about our church and our community. Not because they don't want to do it themselves but because they feel my Mandarin is better than theirs. Also, I have been with the church since I was two years old and I know it quite well. We are a small Korean minority community of about eighty families. There is a much larger one some fifty kilometres away with over 400 families. In our case, we are all Christians. The heads of the households make a solemn pledge every year at Easter that our whole village will live for ever in devotion to our Lord Jesus Christ. Then it is the young people's turn. Last year, the weather was freezing. Nevertheless, we had our traditional Easter outdoor service early in the morning. It was still dark; I could not count the number of people there. We could not sing at all; it was too cold. We raised high our arms and prayed, received special blessings from the elders and returned to our homes.

Pastor John Tsai has been our pastor for many years. He's been with us right from the beginning. For the past three years, however, he has not been able to leave his house, so he blesses the buns and the wine, and the deacons carry them into the church, and we have the fellowship of the holy communion. We have fixed a loudspeaker in his room so he can follow the service. We have a big room across the open courtyard, capable of seating sixty people along the four walls. Other people bring small wooden stools, so we can seat about 120 altogether in three rows all around. We have been thinking of putting in benches, but wood is difficult to come by.

Pastor Tsai is not Korean, he is a Han. I was told that he used to work with the big church in Shenyang. But when the Korean church fell into difficulties with the authorities in 1952, Pastor Tsai helped work things out, and so, when one day our Korean friends introduced him to us, we welcomed him. He's been pastor at our church since then. Pastor Tsai's wife died in the late sixties. I was only six, but I took part in the mourning and comforting week; I was in charge of providing hot tea to those who came in to sit with Pastor Tsai. If it had not been for Pastor Tsai's insistence, it would have gone on beyond the one week. Pastor Tsai is that much respected in the community. Of his three sons, two are working elsewhere and have their families, but they come back at the New Year; the middle one died in the Korean War.

About eight years ago, Lee Big Sister came to us from Korea where she had been ministering to Christian groups. As we grew in number and saw Pastor Tsai's health beginning to fail, we contacted our friends and relatives in Korea and were able to get her to come over and serve us.

Our village community, I am told, began in the early years of the century when many Koreans were brought in by the Japanese to work in the new steel mills and, farther north, in the timber industries. Some were lucky to have their families with them, some joined them later. Some married local girls. But from the start, even up to the Liberation, relationships between us and the Han people were not good. You see, we were brought in to work in the mills because the Japanese did not trust the Hans at the time. And, of course, Koreans did not like the Hans either. They would not let us move into the town. And so we had our settlement here. But now the town has extended itself, and so we are very much part of it. After the Liberation, we received much better treatment. The cadres were kind to us: after all we belong to China and many were born here. We were also given train tickets to pay short visits to our relatives and when we got into the train, we found gift parcels of food and fruits on the seats.

The American war in Korea was bad. Our motherland was almost swallowed up by the Americans until Chairman Mao permitted volunteers to move across the river border. To be sure, the Party gave us support. A lot of Chinese volunteered, and of course our community did. My father said some fifty young Korean men went to fight. Ten did not return, not even their bone ashes. The families received medals and a sum of money. Today some of us still hate American imperialists.

My real father's family name is Tsou. He was a welder. When I was two, he was killed in an accident. My mother, whom I can hardly remember now, wanted very much to go home to her relatives in Korea. But then she probably had to make a child bride of me, otherwise who would want to spend money to feed another family's girl? She did not want to do this. Then my foster parents came along and offered to bring me up, provided I took their name. They had no child of their own, and their wanting me to carry their name guaranteed that I would not be made a child bride. So my mother agreed and went home. She did not write back. A few years later word came through that she had married, and wanted me to be obedient to my foster parents.

My foster parents are very kind people. Both are deeply pious Christians. As an elder, my father is one of the leaders of the church and of the community. One of his tasks is to see to it that parents bring up their children in the Christian way. He is so conscientious that at one time he had a class at home for young parents on Christian parenthood. He still takes special pains to call in the young people to have long talks with them. His other regular task is the morning prayer at 6:30 every day for some twenty families in the neighbourhood. Normally four or five show up, sometimes ten. I did not attend until I was fifteen. My father is a very different person when he is praying. Normally he is very strict, and capable. People come to him for all kinds of advice. But when praying, he is much gentler, and he does not scold people.

One of our present problems is who our next pastor should be. The people do not agree. Some want a man. Some feel that after so many years of faithful service, Lee Big Sister ought to be made pastor. These people point out that women pastors are not uncommon. My father has not said much on the subject. My feeling is he is probably in favour of having a man. Pastor Tsai stayed away from the discussion. He would like to see us consult other Christian people in the province.

Three years ago, our church had a terrible time. Elder Chong, one of the oldest of the elders, was accused by his unit (in the steel plant) of conspiracy to default. Apparently, as a top engineering worker, he had managerial responsibilities. As they were going through the books they found a lot of irregularities. Elder Chong wanted to speak to the church after a Sunday service. So we ate our hot noodles as we listened to him. He said that he had not cheated. He had no extra money. (My father confirmed that.) But very probably there were irregularities for which he could be held responsible. His wife angrily jumped up and defended him. She said that during the Cultural Revolution, it would be irregular not to have irregularities. It was a time of power play and her husband was a victim. It was a very emotional meeting. Elder Chong and his associates rose from many quarters. Most of the church people were behind him, but a number wavered. After some months, Elder Chong was demoted by four points at his job, and that was the end of the story. It was completely unjust. Nobody knew what actually happened; certainly not a young girl like me. I respect him as an elder. He is always an elder to me.

My father told me specifically to tell our evangelism story. Eight or nine years ago, our village was not all Christian. My blood mother was not a Christian. We had a lot of problems among us. Some wives are of Korean blood, some Han. One of the problems, I understand, had to do with coke. We depend on coke for fuel to keep our room warm. It so happened that the Korean women felt that the Han women were getting better quality coke, in bigger pieces and at the same price, thanks to their family ties with those in charge. This was the beginning. Soon the men were drawn in. It was bad. People did not talk to each other.

The crisis came during an extremely cold winter. A baby boy died in the night. The mother almost went crazy. She made wild accusations regarding the quality of the coke and why it went dead in the middle of the night. Things became very tense. The heads of the families came together to deal with the accusation and find a solution to the matter of coke distribution. There were Christians on both sides. For some time, the discussion got nowhere. Then Brother Lee, whose wife is Han, volunteered to share his coke with others. Nobody took him seriously. But he did what he promised. After work hours, he would bring a few kilos of coke and give it to a Korean family. Nobody know what game he was playing. He simply walked in, gave his greetings and said: 'I've come to see if you need coke. This is fine coke.' If there was no response, he would simply leave the coke by the stove and go away. Sometimes they would examine the coke, chat about its quality and have tea. One Sunday, after the service, Elder Chong asked Brother Lee to come up. He embraced him in front of everybody, and told the church what Brother Lee had done. He said: 'Brother Lee alone acted like our Lord. He showed us the way.' Brother Lee was moved to tears. Elder Chong could not contain himself either. Soon everybody was crying and confessing their sins to each other.

Evangelism is very important for us. Father insists that it must begin with the heads of families; otherwise, he reasons, what right does he have to be the family head? So he puts in a lot of effort as an elder to get parents to be good Christians and to teach their wives and children about God. When it's his turn to preach, he likes to ask the people to commit themselves to preaching the gospel to their neighbours. He would ask people to raise their hands, he would have a young man take down their names. Later in the week, or the next Sunday, he would get hold of these people one by one and ask them how they were faring.

63

Set Apart

Raymond Fung

It is not easy for Christians from the outside world to understand this. But a long while ago, we made a decision to be a holy people, setting ourselves apart for the cause of the gospel. This means, among other things, that we will not be part of the Three Self Movement nor will we take part in public Sunday services, no matter what. I guess you can call us an underground church, the way you were met by one of us near the bus stop and brought here in a roundabout way.

I have been made the Responsible Brother for a period of three years. This is my second term. To fulfil my God-given task, I gave up my job as an accountant, and devoted myself full-time to the care of the church. My brothers and sisters take care of my needs. We tithe. That's something we commit ourselves to. There are fourteen of us, myself included. We have enough.

As the Responsible Brother, my tasks are four, very clearly defined.

1. I pray. About two hours each day, I pray for each member of the church by name. I lift them up to God for grace and strength.

2. I study the Scripture another two to three hours. Every week I give a 45-minute to one-hour 'light from the scriptures' Bible study after worship.

3. I examine the faith of the believers. At least twice a month, I am required to get together with each church member for an hour, usually two to three hours, for an examination of the heart. Here we go into matters of the soul and of the spirit. We talk and pray and struggle together. I have authority to demand submission.

4. I attend a church council meeting once a month in which I am questioned by all members of the church about my work, my spiritual state, and the affairs of the church. They can ask any question they want to about me, and I must expose myself totally in front of my brothers and sisters. They can also make public confession if the Spirit moves them.

With regard to worship, you have now attended one service. Brother Chang and two others are in charge. He is a waterworks worker. At the service, I cease to be the Responsible Brother. Before the direct presence of God, every one is equal. After the service, I give my Bible message.

Every worship is a communion service: Christ speaking to his disciples. That is why we have a twenty-minute period of silence before communion. Any one of us can break bread. Brother Chang gives the assignment. The service is simple, we expose ourselves before God in hymns, and silence, and meet him in the communion and Bible exegesis. I hope you are not offended at not being allowed to take part in communion with us. But I'm sure you shared our spirit.

Most of us in the church have our Christian roots in the indigenous Chinese Christian movement, perhaps most obviously identifiable with Teacher Wang Ming Tao. We are not Little Flock. We are not Baptist. I guess we are less sectarian than the former, and less activist and noisy than the latter.

It is true we have not been evangelizing very well. Since 1975, when we got ourselves organized again, only three have joined us, while we lost two through death and three to Hong Kong. They joined their families. It worried us but not too greatly. Christian faithfulness must come first. We have long decided not to compromise in any way in exchange for a more relaxed life. We must be faithful to God's call for holiness. 'Be ye separated.'

This is why we want no part of the public Sunday services. It pains me to see many of God's servants give up their principles and go the easy way. I do not question their faith, but it's the wrong setting, the wrong circumstances. It is one thing to pray and preach. And quite another thing to pray and preach under the so-called tolerance of an atheistic power. To participate in that is to participate in a clown show. There is no option for us but to separate ourselves for holiness. Times are bad. Christians must prepare for all eventualities.

With regard to the Three Self Movement, I would only say that the believer and the non-believer do not share the same yoke. Their sermons may sound evangelical, but they don't mean it. It is all a show in concert with the Religious Affairs Bureau and in pursuit of their goal of religious control.

I am not a political man. I support the People's Government as everybody does. But as a Christian, I can have no consort with atheistic communism. No Christian in close fellowship with God would or could do so without losing his soul. I know that while a number of famous evangelical pastors are also members of the Three Self Movement Committee now, God only knows why. But God would always leave behind his faithful to bear his name. We hope we are worthy. The only important thing for a Christian is to be constantly in Christ, hidden in him, to appreciate his glory and beauty, worship him, enjoy him, and look forward to his coming in the fullness of his glory.

You ask me about the three new members. Sau Lin is twenty-six, recently married to Brother Chan. We had known of their going out together for months. Brother Chan had been concerned about her salvation. At the time, marriage was out of the question. But Brother Chan prayed. The one day, somehow, the Holy Spirit moved Sau Lin to seek me out. We talked for a whole afternoon. She poured out her heart, and confessed Christ on the spot. So we supported the relationship and soon they were married. Sau Lin is new to the faith. She has much to learn.

Another of the three, Tso, has been with us for two years. He's an Indonesian Chinese, stuck here permanently because he could not go back to Indonesia, and Hong Kong would not have him. He has no work, no family. His wife left him some years back. Now he depends entirely on transfers from his parents in Java. I saw him several times in a nearby park in the morning, just sitting around and reading newspapers, doing nothing. Finally I approached him and immediately he hung on to me and told me everything. He was so lonely he had almost gone crazy. At the time, he'd simply given up. He's a skilled electrician. He could have easily got a job, but he could not bring himself to do any organized work. So we talked and I led him to Christ. After some time, we welcomed him to our fellowship. His is one of the sad stories of our time. He had left Indonesia for China in 1962, like many Indonesian Chinese at the time. He wanted to be involved in the construction of a socialist society here. He spent two years in a technical institute, did well in both technical and political studies. He got an important maintenance job. He got married. But he was never fully accepted by his colleagues. Maybe it had to do with his having money from abroad, which automatically lifted him up above many others. Of course foreign exchange became a dirty word in the Cultural Revolution. Then his wife left him. He became depressed. He applied for a visa for Hong Kong, gave up his job, and began waiting. I hope his turn will come soon.

Lee Aunt came to us as a result of faithful prayers. She had cancer in the nose. After four months in the hospital, she was sent home to wait for the end. There was nothing more the doctors could do for her, except for a weekly prescription of a pain-killing drug which could only be obtained in the hospital clinic. She was not strong enough to take a bus, so she could not make it. One day, her neighbour, who knew I was a Christian, mentioned her to me, casually wondering 'if religion could do something in that situation'. I don't practise faith healing. I didn't believe or disbelieve in it. I had simply never thought about it. But at that point I felt an obligation to visit the old woman. So I went. She was in pain, crawling in bed. I tried to talk to her about Jesus, about the need for repentance. But I didn't know if she heard me. So I prayed, the only thing I could do. I visited her during the next several days. She was happy I went, but did not respond to anything I did or said. Anyway, before I left, I always prayed with her. And I remember praying for her healing. As she got better, I stopped my visits. The woman gradually disappeared from my mind. Two months later, she found her way to my home, bringing a chicken and half a dozen eggs. They were her gifts to me. She said the doctors told her she's apparently all right now. The cancer in the nose seemed to have gone. She was happy and grateful as she fell on her knees before me. I was so frightened I fell on my knees too. We embraced each other. And I thanked God aloud for what he had done.

We do not worry too much about the future of our church. Our mission is to be faithful, whatever the consequences, future or no future. It is in the Lord's hands. We do not care about human judgement. Only God's judgement.

I have not thought much about it, but my hope is that the Lord will return soon, that many may come to know him before it's too late. Maybe through us, or maybe through others.

64

These two prayers were sent to Catholics in Hong Kong for daily recitation after the events of 4 June 1989.

Lord God, Creator and Saviour of mankind, please hear the earnest entreaties of your Chinese sons and daughters. Your Holy Son offered his life to save the world, to free people from sin and evil so we can regain freedom. We earnestly beseech you to use the power of the Holy Spirit to free the Chinese people from danger and hardship, that the whole nation from top to bottom may deal with the present situation in a peaceful and intelligent manner. May we at an early date realize democracy, the rule of law and respect for human rights.

Compassionate God, please fill us with the strength of will to bear the hardships of the nation, and to be faithful to the nation and the people. We firmly believe that you are the source of justice and power. You are eternal life and the eternal King. Amen.

God, you determine the course of history, you are the source of justice. Your Holy Son gave his life to save us and deliver us from evil, to regain freedom. We pray for our compatriots who have died, who have given up their lives for the country and the people, for justice, democracy and freedom. Lord, please graciously examine their sacrifice and as your Holy Son promised, if a grain does not die it abides alone, but if it dies it multiplies a hundred times. We beg you to receive them into eternal life, and we ask you to inspire the sons and daughters of China with enthusiasm, that they may abandon hatred and full of determination fight to the end together with the people. May we repair the damage, implement democracy and the rule of law as soon as possible. Lord, we beg you to save our compatriots, to liberate them from tyranny soon. Through our Lord Jesus Christ with you and the Holy Spirit, the only God, eternal King. Amen.

65

Statement by hunger strikers from institutions of higher education in Beijing, Tiananmen Square, May 1989.

Democracy is the most noble feeling in human existence and freedom is a God given human right for all people. Surely it is not something for the Chinese people to be proud of that we must lose our young lives to gain these things? We are not pleased to go on hunger strike for these demands, yet we have no alternative. We are ready to fight to the death for the sake of the living. But we are still children, we are still children! Mothers of China, please take a look at your sons and daughters: surely you cannot remain indifferent when our young lives are cruelly threatened, when death is approaching. We do not want to die, we certainly want to lead a good life, since we are in the flower of our youth. We do not want to die, we want to study well. The country is so poor, we certainly do not want to die and leave the country in this state. But if the death of one person or of a few people can make many others live better, can make the country glorious and prosperous, then we have no right to prolong an ignoble existence.

Recommended Reading

A number of church groups have run substantial programmes of research, documentation and publication on Christianity in China. Here it is only possible to mention some of the most important. In Hong Kong, *Bridge* and *Ching Feng* report church news and theological debate from an ecumenical perspective; *Tripod* is a Catholic journal; the Chinese Church Research Center and Asian Outreach International report on China from an evangelical standpoint, sometimes very critical of official Church organizations. The Urban University of Rome, Chinese Catholic Communications (Singapore) and Pro Mundi Vita (Louvain) have all produced useful material on Chinese Catholicism. Articles on China also appear regularly in *Missiology* and *Religion in Communist Lands*. An excellent source of information and comment is the *China Study Project Journal*. The China Study Project is a British ecumenical initiative which since 1976 has collated reference material on government policy, church activities etc., and moreover has closely monitored developments in Buddhism, Islam and Taoism. Issues of the journal also include longer interpretative articles.

Several recent books can be strongly recommended. *Unfinished Encounter — China and Christianity* (Collins, 1988) by Bob Whyte (Project Officer of the China Study Project from 1975 to 1986) provides an overview of Christianity in China from early times through to the 1980s, with more than half the book focusing on the post-1949 period. It is excellently written and a mine of solidly researched information. Another major work is Philip Wickeri, *Seeking the Common Ground — Protestant Christianity, The Three-Self Movement and China's United Front* (Orbis Books, 1988), which focuses on the TSPM from its formation in the 1950s until the present, providing a comprehensive treatment of CCP policy on the united front and religion, the Protestant response and the establishment of a 'working relationship' between Christians and Communists.

Wise As Serpents, Harmless as Doves by Chao and van Houten (William Carey Library, 1988) is a very different kind of book, reporting transcribed interviews with Christians in evangelical sects. Here the voices speak a language totally different from that of the sophisticated urban élite and national Church leaders. The book offers fascinating glimpses of Christianity at village level, with an emphasis on healing and miracles, together with some moving personal histories. The book also contains a useful introduction by Jonathan Chao on state/Church relations 1949–88.

Towards a Contextual Ecclesiology (Phototech Systems, 1987) by Kim-Kwong Chan focuses on the Catholic Church in the early 1980s — relations with the state, with the Vatican, theological issues, ecclesiology, internal structure and daily practices. It also contains a detailed analysis of CCP religious policy since 1949.

More popular books on the Chinese Church include Leslie Lyall's *Come Wind, Come Weather* (London: Hodder & Stoughton, 1960); *New Spring in China* (London: Hodder & Stoughton, 1979); and *God Reigns in China* (London: Hodder & Stoughton, 1985). Raymond Fung's *Households of God* (Geneva: World Council of Churches, 1982) collects many testimonies of Christian communities in China, especially during times of persecution. *Claws of the Dragon* (Grand Rapids, Michigan: Francis Asbury Press, 1988) records the experience of a Chinese Christian during the Cultural Revolution. Britt E. Towery Jr's *The Churches of China: Taking Root Downward, Bearing Fruit Upward* (Hong Kong: Amazing Grace Books Ltd, 1986) and David H. Adeney's *China: The Church's Long March: Experience of God in Church* (London: OMF, 1988) provide good surveys of the Church in China. Arthur Wallis's *China Miracle: A Voice to the Church in the West* (London: Kingsway Publications Ltd, 1985), suggests that the West can learn many valuable lessons from the experiences of the Chinese Church.